With love, I dedicate this book to my wife, Susan
and our son, Jay.

Care of the
Elderly

FEBRUARY 1999

Dr R. B. Shukla

M.B.B.S., M.D., F.R.C.P.I.

Consultant Physician (Locum),

University Hospital of South Manchester (NHS Trust)

Withington Hospital,

Burton House,

Nell·Lane,

Manchester M20 2LR

UK

London: The Stationery Office

ISBN 0 11 702334 5

Published by The Stationery Office and available from:

The Publications Centre
(mail, telephone and fax orders only)
PO Box 276, London SW8 5DT
General enquiries 0171 873 0011
Telephone orders 0171 873 9090
Fax orders 0171 873 8200

The Stationery Office Bookshops
123 Kingsway, London WC2B 6PQ
0171 242 6393 Fax 0171 242 6394
68–69 Bull Street, Birmingham B4 6AD
0121 236 9696 Fax 0121 236 9699
33 Wine Street, Bristol BS1 2BQ
0117 926 4306 Fax 0117 929 4515
9–21 Princess Street, Manchester M60 8AS
0161 834 7201 Fax 0161 833 0634
16 Arthur Street, Belfast BT1 4GD
01232 238451 Fax 01232 235401
The Stationery Office Oriel Bookshop
18–19 High Street, Cardiff CF1 2BZ
01222 395548 Fax 01222 384347
71 Lothian Road, Edinburgh EH3 9AZ
0131 228 4181 Fax 0131 622 7017

The Stationery Office's Accredited Agents
(see Yellow Pages)

and through good booksellers

Contents

DR R. B. Shukla

Dr R. B. Shukla qualified in Medicine from Prince of Wales Medical College, Patna (Patna University), India, in 1962 and acquired M.D. in General Medicine in 1966. He came to the UK in 1969 and has served in the National Health Service ever since.

A General Practitioner turned Geriatrician, he has worked as Consultant Physician in Medicine for the Elderly at North Manchester General Hospital from 1982, from where he took early retirement in 1996. Currently, he is working as Consultant Geriatrician (Locum) at University Hospital of South Manchester (Withington Hospital, Manchester) His clinical responsibilities have included general care of the elderly, stroke rehabilitation, Parkinson's Disease, hypertension, cardiac failure, orthopaedic/geriatric rehabilitation and osteoporosis. While his research interests include falls in the elderly and drug treatment in the elderly, his general interests are in the fields of housing for the elderly and retirement. A Fellow of the Royal College of Physicians of Ireland (FRCPI) since 1990, Dr Shukla has several publications to his credit.

PREFACE to the second edition

Happily, the Second Edition of this book coincides with the pre-millennium year, 1999, which has been declared International Year of the Elderly Persons by the United Nations. The chapters have been thoroughly revised. Also, several new chapters have been added – on Ischaemic Heart Disease, Infection, Management of Headaches, Parkinson's Disease; Fits, Faints and Funny Turns; Aches and Pains, Pins and Needles; Management of Cancers and Rational Prescribing in the Elderly. With the exception of chapters on Management of Cancer, Ischaemic Heart Disease, Stroke and Community Care – which are described in detail – other chapters have been written in a general way.

It is hoped that like the first edition, the book will appeal to a large readership – from final year medical students and House Officers to therapists, nurses, social workers and managers, (both of hospitals and that of nursing homes). Every effort has been made to explain medical terms and abbreviations and to avoid medical jargon. Useful addresses and Reading Lists have been inserted at the end of each chapter. There is also a selected list of helpful publications at the end of the book, both for Professionals and other readers. To make the book more readable, useful information – 'fillers' – has been included in between most chapters. All in all, it is hoped that the book will also be useful, as before, to lay members of the public.

Acknowledgements

I am very grateful to several colleagues for their help and encouragement in preparing this edition. They include Dr Elaine Young (for her chapter on Management of Cancers), Dr Kate Williamson (for her help in the preparation of the chapter on Ischaemic Heart Disease), Dr Bernard Perera (for his contribution in the chapter on Infection) and Mrs Dorothy Phillips, Social Worker for her considerable contribution to the chapter on Community Care.

I am extremely grateful to Professor Peter Millard for his helpful criticisms of the manuscripts. My Secretary Judith Cairns of The Royal Oldham Hospital deserves special mention and my unqualified thanks for her time, skill and loyalty while preparing the manuscripts.

Finally, I offer my sincere thanks to the Publishers, The Stationery Office and their Officers, Richard Middleton, Miss Helen Bodenham and Mrs Valerie Taylor.

Dr R. B. Shukla
Manchester, UK
February 1999.

Introduction

CHAPTER 1

The care of elderly people is going to be a big challenge as we approach the 21st century. This is mainly due to demographic changes (combination of both decreasing fertility and increasing longevity) and the effect of the baby boom generation, following the Second World War, with its retirement age early in the 21st century. These challenges will apply not only to this and other industrialised countries but also to developing countries. In the next two to three decades the population of old people in developing countries is likely to double. This will put tremendous strain on their meagre health and social services' resources. In developed countries, where the challenges of ageing are well recognised, the need for the care of the elderly – especially those who are very old – will increase further. Thus, while in 1952 one person reached one hundred years old every other day; in 1999 it was five people a day and in the year 2010 it is estimated to increase to 20 daily. Japan is likely to have a major share of this challenge among the industrialised countries as it is estimated that 25 per cent of its population will be over 65 by the year 2025.

So who are the elderly? The term elderly is usually used for a person at or above their retirement age. In the UK, this is 60 years or above in women and 65 years or above in men.

This definition of 'elderly' is clearly unsatisfactory. It has been suggested that the term 'young elderly' should be used for those between 65 and 75 years and 'old elderly' for those beyond 75 years. This is especially in view of the fact that we are now living longer – in 1945, life expectancy was 66 years for men and 71 for women; in 1999 it is 74 years for men and 79 for women. To be realistic, I would even go on to suggest that no one should be called elderly below 80 years of age.

A larger proportion of women than men suffer from diseases in their later life, as women tend to outlive their husbands.

Taking the UK as a whole, with its population of over 56 million, over 15 per cent of the people are aged 65 or above. As 94 per cent of the elderly population live in the community, the various members of the Primary Care Team (General Practitioners, District Nurses, Social Workers, Physiotherapists, Occupational Therapists, etc.) have a major role to play in the welfare of the elderly. However, the Departments of Medicine for the Elderly up and down the country have provided immense opportunities for acute therapeutic intervention in elderly patients.

What are the challenges?

It must be clearly understood that ageing is not a disease; it is a normal phenomenon. It should be our aim to make old age – almost one-third of total lifespan – enjoyable.

Ageing as such is not the cause of the problems encountered by the elderly. It is only when physical, mental and social factors, either singly or in combination, interact with the effects of ageing (poor balance, to give an example,) that the problems arise.

It should be realised that diseases can present differently in the elderly compared with young people. Hence, their recognition may pose problems. For example, a 'heart attack' may not occur with chest pain but can occur with falls and possible confusion. Besides, elderly people may suffer from more than one disease.

To make matters worse, some symptoms or signs may be due to several diseases or pathologies. For example, poor mobility in an elderly lady can be due to marked curvature of the spine, partial blindness, old stroke and most likely, general frailty.

A functional assessment in all cases is a must, even after correct identification of all disease in the patient.

So what are the main problems faced by our elderly patient? They are many, and include falls, confusional states, depression, urinary incontinence, backache and difficulty in swallowing, to name but a few. Out of these, take an example of dementia. Ten per cent of the aged over 65 develop this disease, increasing to 20 per cent of those over 80 years of age.

What needs to be done?

In a short article like this it is not possible to suggest all the remedies. I can only highlight the following:

1. Good *communication* between various members of the Primary Care Team, local Adult Medicine/ Geriatric Units, Local Authorities and voluntary organisations should be a must to make the most of the available resources. Sometimes inappropriate referrals are due to poor communication between general practitioners and hospital doctors. (Please see Chapter 18 on Communication.)

2. *Early referral* of elderly patients to specialist units, such as geriatric or psychogeriatric units, is essential to prevent them becoming long-stay patients. In this respect, the general practitioners should enlist the help of the District Nurses and Health Visitors.

3. *Appropriate staffing* of Nursing Homes and Old People's Homes is another area which should be looked into. There should be more nursing and rehabilitation staff input in these homes. Many admissions in local hospitals, where beds are already at a premium, are mainly on nursing grounds. It is no joy to frail, elderly patients to move from these homes to hospital and back. Also, more and more confused patients are being admitted to these homes.

It is therefore, only sensible to appoint staff who have the know-how for these patients.

Sooner or later, I feel, we shall have to change our present habit of putting unwilling elderly in impersonal homes. There are some attractive alternatives. Boarding them out with people who care, is one of the many options. It is hoped that when Community Care finally takes full effect in a few years, similar problems will be largely eliminated.

4. *Inappropriate drug therapy* in the elderly patient is not only wasteful but may make their lives miserable by causing side effects which are very com-

mon in the elderly. Prescribing prochlorperazine (Stemetil) in elderly patients, for giddiness due to age-related loss of postural stability, should be deprecated.

5. *Violence* towards the elderly. It is usual these days to read in the newspapers or to see on the television that one of the elderly – many of them frail and defenceless – has been attacked. It is the duty of us all, not only the police or the social workers, to feel bound to help prevent such devastating crises.

6. *Rationing.* This has been the subject of debate and discussion both in lay press and medical circles. Whatever the reason may be, rationing should not be made on the basis of age alone, although it has to be said that some sort of rationing is now unavoidable generally as it is impossible to provide all the health care one needs, especially in the current cash-controlled climate.

7. *Emergency admissions.* These have almost reached crisis point during the past few years. There are various reasons for this. These include:

a.) Inadequate number of beds due to bed reductions in hospitals.

b.) Diminished support in the community, including help from Social Services.

c.) More elderly people needing medical attention.

d.) Increased patients' (relatives') awareness in matters concerning health and there is nothing wrong with this, I hasten to add!

So what changes have taken place and which are going to take place?

1. In hospitals, integration of geriatric Medicine with General Medicine in its various forms has taken place and is continuing.

2. Continuing care of elderly patients is taking place more and more in private nursing homes and more General Practitioners are supervising them.

3. The Royal Commission on the funding of long-term care has already been announced and the findings were announced in March 1999 (see Chapter 20 on Community Care).

4. The House Of Commons Health Select Committee is considering the interface between Health and Social Services (*B.G.S. News,* January 1998) and The British Geriatric Society is taking an active interest in this.

5. There have been calls for legislation to outlaw ageism.

6. A 'Pensioner's Task Force' has recently been instituted by this Government.

The changes announced by this Government for pensioners during the latest (July 1998) spending review (e.g. (a) guaranteeing a minimum weekly income of £75 for all single Pensioners and £116 for a couple, (b) recruitment of Personal Advisers to ensure that the poorest Pensioners claim and receive the welfare benefits to which they are entitled, (c) abolition of eye-test charges, (d) concessionary travel plans etc.) are to be welcomed and are 'steps in the right direction', as generally speaking, the longer we live, the poorer we become.

So what should the doctors (and other professionals) engaged in the care of the elderly do?

The answer is to continue following the ten golden principles:

1. The diagnosis in an elderly patient should be arrived at after considering the triad of physical, mental (and psychological) and social circumstances of the patient. Besides, one must be very patient whilst making diagnoses, i.e. whilst taking history and examining the patient.

2. Disease presentation in the elderly may be unusual. Also, presentation may be non-specific even in serious diseases and therefore, treatment should not be delayed.

3. Multiple pathologies should always be considered. Also, one symptom could be due to several pathologies or causes (e.g. falls, giddiness).

4. A pathology should be correlated with a disease rather than with the patient's age. Also, treatment should not be based on age alone.

5. Recognise patients with maximum risk: frail, living alone, with a history of fall/confusion/incontinence/depression/bereavement and especially if they are 'old elderly' i.e. over 80–85 years.

6. Utmost care should be taken in drug prescribing in the elderly – necessity of prescribing drugs, their side effects, interactions and contra-indications. Polypharmacy should be avoided. Although older people – those over 65 – account for only 18 per cent of the population, they receive half of all medicines prescribed. (*British Medical Journal* 10 May 1997).

7. Rehabilitation by multidisciplinary team is at the heart of management of elderly patients. Where necessary, activities of daily living should be assessed.

8. One should be aware of common medical problems such as ischaemic heart disease, strokes, prostatism, constipation, falls, deafness, cancer, depression, dementia and osteoporosis etc.

9. Social needs of elderly patients should form part and parcel of overall medical management:

a.) Assess and if necessary, provide social care

b.) Carers should not be forgotten

10. Lastly, it is vital that adequate communication be made with patients and their relatives regarding aspects of care, including written instructions and leaflets etc.

Although the words of Aneurin Bevan (the founder of the National Health Service) – "we never shall have all we need" – are true even today, the elderly people deserve the best treatment and care we can give them. Examples include:

1. Arthritis of the hip causes considerable pain and disability, more so in elderly patients. Many such patients can be relieved of their misery by hip replacement operations. In the UK 20,000 hip replacements are done every year. After all, none other than the Queen Mother had this operation not long ago at the age of 95.

2. Heart rhythm disturbances, especially complete heart block, can be effectively treated by a permanent pacemaker, thus preventing an elderly patient from having symptoms such as giddiness, fall, bouts of unconsciousness, or even death.

Death and dying

We all have to die one day – there comes a time when death becomes an essential part of life. Many readers may have watched the excellent series, The Human Body, on BBC Television. In its last episode (June 25, 1998), the words of Herbie (a German in his 60s living with his wife in the West of Ireland, and his health deteriorating from an inoperable tumour in the stomach), still haunt me: "I want everyone to see that a human being can manage an illness like my illness . . . that there is a way to make the best of the end of your life". Thus, our ability to face our own death is most remarkable and must be one of the greatest human attributes. It is the duty of doctors and others involved to make this 'end of life' as comfortable and as humane as possible.

Finally, it is worth mentioning BGS (British Geriatrics Society) and Age Concern, the two national organisations who stand out among several organisations concerned directly or indirectly for improving the overall care of the elderly population:

1. *The British Geriatrics Society* (BGS) was founded in 1947 for "the relief of suffering and distress amongst the aged and infirm by the improvement of standards of medical care for such persons, the holdings of meetings and the publication and distribution of the results of research".

The Society is the only professional association of doctors practising geriatric medicine. The 1800 members world-wide are consultants in Geriatric Medicine, the psychiatry of old age, public health medicine, general practitioners and scientists engaged in the research of age-related diseases. The Society works closely with medical and voluntary bodies concerned with the medicine of old age and care of older people.

2. *Age Concern England* is the leading charitable movement in the United Kingdom concerned with ageing and older people. It has 1400 local groups which are supported by 250,000 volunteers and provides community-based services such as luncheon clubs, day centres and home-visiting. Age Concern has been taking a lead role nationally in research, specialist information and advice provision, Parliamentary work, policy analysis, publishing and last but not least, campaigning.

Sir Ronald Gibson, during his address to the Royal Society of Medicine several years ago observed: "The care of the elderly is a scandal, and a system by which these vulnerable citizens are managed or manipulated is a disgrace. It is becoming nothing less than a national crisis". Our standard of care for the elderly must rise to such a level as to make such statements unnecessary. Besides, even if death is inevitable, disability may not be – so neither the young nor the old should accept the present ageing pattern as immutable.

Useful addresses

British Geriatrics Society,
1 St. Andrews Place,
Regents Park, London NW1 4LB
Tel: 0171 935 4004

Age Concern
Age Concern England,
Astral House,
1268 London Road,
London SW16 4ER
Tel: 0181 679 8000; Fax 0181 679 6069

(Please see list of publications by Age Concern at the end of the book)

References/Further reading list

1. *Why Survive? Being Old in America* by Robert N. Butler, Harper and Row, 1975

2. Introduction, in *Oxford Text of Geriatric Medicine.* OUP, 1992

3. *Rationing: Talk and Action in Health Care.* (Ed. Bill New). Co-published by the King Fund and B.M.J. Publishing Group, November 1997

4. *British Geriatric Society's Compendium,* 2nd Edition, 1997

5. *The Times;* July 18, 1998

Who is Elderly?

" The arbitrary definition of the state of being 'geriatric' beginning at age 65 or 75 is an historical accident and while it may have administrative convenience, it has no basis in biology or epidemiology, and may not always be in the best interest of older people. The processes that lead to disease and disability in old age are life long and can only be understood and modified through a life-long perspective on ageing."

(Source: Introduction by editors J. Grimley Evans and T. Franklin Williams in their book, *Oxford Text Book of Geriatric Medicine*. OUP 1992)

Retirement

CHAPTER 2

"Work consists of whatever a body is obliged to do, and play consists of whatever a body is obliged not to do" — Mark Twain.

Retirement has become a prominent 'social' phenomenon in a relatively short space of time. It was hardly known at the beginning of the nineteenth century.

The number of people working beyond 65 years has been steadily decreasing – whereas in 1931 over half of the men over 65 were working, the figure was a meagre 19 per cent in 1971 and the corresponding figure must be much lower for 1999.

Retirement has now assumed considerable importance. Why is this so? People are living longer and there is now a trend towards early retirement as people rightly expect years of enjoyable retirement life.

In fact, a man can now expect to live another 15 years or so after retiring at the age of 60, and a woman of the same age, another 19 years.

As is well known, women now have the option either to retire at 60 years or go on working until 65 like their male colleagues.

It is, however, a paradox that people in certain occupations can go on working until they choose to retire; one of the often quoted examples is that of politicians.

Whatever the case may be, a large majority can look forward to their retirement; although for a few, compulsory retirement can be a disaster.

Planning for retirement

During the last decade or so, our attitude towards retirement has changed. More and more people are planning for their retirement. Equally, it appears that more and more people want to retire early rather than late. So the dictum 'work is intrinsically good', may be the motto of the minority of the workers in the coming years.

More people will now like to retire early even if it means paying more in pension contributions.

It is a fact of life that as we grow older we tend to be frailer. "Once a man gets well into his seventies, his existence becomes a mere miracle", observed Robert Louis Stevenson in the late nineteenth century.

Inevitably retirement and subsequent years bring social, economic, psychological and physical problems. Though it would be wrong to blur the picture by these over-simplistic generalisations, the fact is that for the majority, loss of status, income and in many cases companionship, poses a risk to their mental and physical health.

What about initiating or even continuing private medical insurance just in case NHS hospitals may have long waiting lists? In this context it is worth mentioning that there have been rises in medical insurance premiums. There are several reasons for this:

1. Removal of tax relief in the budget, recently
2. Increase in insurance premium tax and
3. Increase in medical inflation costs.

All in all, the elderly (especially those above 80) are hardest hit by this because, in general, the older you are the more likely you are to also become poorer and hence many elderly people may not be able to continue with their private medical insurance premium. One wonders if long-paying loyal customers should have some sort of rebate on premium when they are very old and vulnerable. (*The Times*, June 13 1998)

A number of social agencies and civic groups have organised programmes of employment for retired people. Self-employment and small businesses are popular careers in the post-retirement phase. Employers should not forget the benefits of hiring the experienced older workers.

Where to retire?

This is one of the questions repeatedly asked during pre-retirement courses. It is difficult to give tailored advice as people's situations vary. The decision depends on several factors, such as social and financial situation, proximity of friends and relatives, the sort of house one is living in and so forth.

In general one should think very carefully before moving. The house should ideally be in a safe place, near shops and public buildings and where public transport is easily available.

One very important factor is that children or relatives and friends should be living nearby, if possible. One should also, as far as possible, be able to pursue one's hobby or interests (voluntary work, sport, etc.)

According to Age Concern, many of the United Kingdom's 2.5 million home owners aged over 70 are 'house rich, income poor'. There are schemes for turning some of that capital into cash. This will solve the problem of moving in many cases. Copies of a booklet called 'Using your Home as Capital' can be had from Age Concern England, Astral House, 1268 London Road, London SW16 4ER (June 1998) priced at £4.99.

It must be said, however, that more counselling and information regarding housing should be made available for couples nearing retirement.

Enjoy yourself

Retirement is usually thought to be a period of rest and leisure. One can achieve this by keeping active. Happily there is little evidence that retirement by itself produces quick changes in one's physical well-being.

The greatest threat seems to be psychological. Loneliness could be a big problem and there comes the need for friends and relatives.

During our younger days, we may not need as many friends but as we grow older, the need for many new friends grows. We should, therefore, make new acquaintances and cement old ones.

One does not have to go to town to do this, as one only has to look around to achieve this – neighbours, colleagues at work and old friends, for example.

Long-lasting friendship needs more lubrication than merely writing two dozen or so cards during the Christmas period to one's friends, relatives and well-wishers.

Besides, one should have friendship with younger people who can help actively in times of need.

Keeping active does not necessarily mean digging the garden daily. One can enjoy a holiday which one did not have time to go on previously. Some holiday firms cater for retired people. Several options are open for pursuing hobbies like writing a book, ballroom dancing, or bird watching.

All in all it would not be an exaggeration to suggest that for many retired people, life may begin at 60 or even 65.

Pre-Retirement Association

Pre-Retirement Association (PRA) is the central pre-retirement body in the country. It is an educational charity which promotes preparation for retirement and provides lectures, and seminars to different groups (i.e. companies, public bodies, etc.) concerned with problems of impending retirement.

There are pre-retirement groups locally all over the country, and they are all affiliated to a central body in London (please see address at the end of this chapter).

The preparation for retirement is multi-faceted and may involve changes in attitude. With this in mind the PRA helps individuals to cope with impending retirement by encouraging employers, local education authorities or indeed other community-based organisations to provide suitable opportunities for preparation. The PRA is closely associated with a helpful and enjoyable monthly magazine *Choice*.

The preparation for retirement courses covers various aspects of retired persons' needs, i.e. home (heating, lighting, insulation), finances (planning retirement budgets), leisure pursuits, holidays, health and diet.

Pre-retirement classes should be attended by more and more people approaching their retirement, though it has to be said that not everyone needs retirement lectures.

ARP (Association of Retired Persons) over 50

Over 120,000 people have joined this Association since its inception in 1988. It represents 18 million people over 50 in the United Kingdom. It is self-helped.

The development of satisfying interests, hobbies and alternative occupations should be considered well in advance. More often than not, a person who has enjoyed his work, will enjoy his retirement too.

There are plenty of things – and many of these do not cost a lot of money – that one can do in retirement to enjoy oneself.

Retirement should not be considered to be a period of rest and leisure only. To enjoy one's retirement one should keep both physically and mentally active. Any exercise or activity should be realistic and should be gradually built up. Clearly, a person who has no previous interest in walking should not aim to walk long distances only a few days after starting to walk. It is encouraging to note that more retired people are now taking part in various sports activities such as golf, and becoming members of Gyms and Health Clubs.

More and more mature people are now registering for part-time degrees in arts and illustration. In fact in visual art, a person's maturity and long experience is a definite advantage. Mature people retain their interest in such activities although they may get tired. The reverse, however, seems to be the case regarding young people – they burn out, although they may not get tired.

A positive attitude to life is essential and one should enjoy, where possible, every moment of one's life.

Finally, when retired and old, people do expect adulation and where possible this should be provided to them. When asked why he had not considered angling after retirement, Bob Hope replied, "Fish do not applaud" !

Useful Address

The Pre-Retirement Association of Great Britain & Ireland,
19 Undine Street,
London SW17 8PP
Tel No: 0171 767 3225

References/Further reading list

1. *Work and Retirement*, Stanley Parker. George Allen & Unwin Ltd., 1982

2. *The Elderly at Home*, A. Hunt, HMSO 1978

3. *A Guide to Care of the Elderly* (Eds. R.B. Shukla and D. Brooks) - Chapter on Retirement, HMSO 1996

4. *Increasing Longevity – Medical, Social and Political Implications*, (Ed. Raymond Tallis) The Royal College of Physicians. ISBN I 86016 0778

5. Views and Reviews, *British Medical Journal* Vol. 317, 8 August, 1998 issue, Page 419.

6. *Enjoy your Later Life*: *Physical and Emotional Wellbeing* for Older Women (series of 25 fact sheets such as exercise, healthy eating, accident prevention, emotional and mental health). Available from Department of Health, P.O. Box 410, Wetherby, West Yorks, LS23 7LN. (Fax 0990 210 266)

Give Elderly People Their Due

..."I would like to urge acceptance of the Rule of Three in Ten. This stern law, insists that, on any committee or board or council, there should be three people over sixty for every ten members. That is the demographic litmus-test".

[Source: Eric Midwinter in, *Age – The Unrecognised Discrimination* (Ed. Evelyn McEwen). Age Concern (1990)]

Managing Ischaemic Heart Disease

CHAPTER 3

Words and Abbreviations used:

HDL = High density lipoproteins, Bi-basal = base of both lungs, MI = Myocardial Infarction (or heart attack)

LDL = Low density lipoproteins, BP = blood pressure, Hyperglycaemia = raised blood-sugar

Ischaemic heart disease is the biggest killer in the Western World, starting from the fourth decade onwards as its incidence rises with age.

Presentation of ischaemic heart disease in the elderly

Apart from 'typical' presentation with severe chest pain, other presentations include chest discomfort, falls, confusional state, arrhythmias (irregular heart rhythm), 'silent' heart attack (i.e. only electrocardiogram reveals the diagnosis) and sudden death.

Causes and risk factors for ischaemic heart disease

Coronary heart disease is multi-factorial. Although preventive measures will delay the symptoms and signs of coronary artery disease, this will not help most people avoid death due to the effect of coronary artery disease. Mechanical blockage of coronary artery due to cholesterol, calcium and fibrous tissue is no longer considered to be the primary manifestation of ischaemic heart disease. It is the disruption of plaque in the coronary artery with associated inflammatory changes which now determines the clinical features of coronary artery disease. Newer developments to deal with the thrombosis include newer antiplatelet agent (glycoprotein 11b/111a receptor antagonist – given intravenously but oral drugs are under trial). Invasive management, i.e. vascularisation, may not be the ideal solution. The various risk factors are:

Blood pressure

Raised blood pressure is an established risk factor for ischaemic heart disease.

Blood pressure levels greater than 160/95 have a two fold increase in ischaemic heart disease.

Smoking

The rate of ischaemic heart disease in smokers is about three times that in non-smokers.

No increased risk is found in those who smoke cigars/pipes, rather than cigarettes.

Blood lipids

The risk of ischaemic heart disease increases with an increase in cholesterol levels. The major atherogenic influence of serum cholesterol is mediated by LDL cholesterol. Serum HDL cholesterol constitutes 20–25% of the serum total cholesterol. It is regarded as the 'protective' cholesterol. Low concentrations of HDL cholesterol are associated with an increased risk of ischaemic heart disease.

Family history

A family history of ischaemic heart disease in a first-degree relative is a risk factor for ischaemic heart disease.

Obesity

Overweight/obese individuals have twice the risk of having a major ischaemic heart disease event.

Physical activity

Sustained regular physical activity is protective against a major ischaemic heart disease event.

Diabetes mellitus

Asymptomatic hyperglycaemia is associated with a twofold increase in the risk of ischaemic heart disease.

Gender

Men aged 33–44 years have an ischaemic heart disease rate five to six times higher than women of the same age. Women are protected by their hormonal functions during menstrual life. This protection is lost during and after the menopause.

Ethnicity

The inhabitants of some countries (e.g. Japan) have a low risk of ischaemic heart disease, but if they migrate to a high risk country, i.e. USA, they show the same rates of ischaemic heart disease as other Americans after several generations.

Stress and type a personality

Strong emotional responses, i.e. stress, may precipitate ischaemic heart disease.

How to make the diagnosis?

Symptoms (what the patient complains of)

Angina is a discomfort in the chest associated with a lack of oxygen to the myocardium (heart muscle) during exercise. Patients often describe a pressure sensation, tightness, squeezing sensation, or a weight on the chest. The pain can radiate to the arms, (especially the left), neck, throat, jaw and back. Other associated features include breathlessness, nausea, vomiting, sweating and dizziness. The pain may abate on rest or taking nitroglycerine. Pain is worsened with exercise. Unstable angina includes patients with:
1. crescendo angina (more severe/frequent attacks)
2. angina at rest/on minimal exertion
3. new onset angina brought on by minimal exertion.

Acute myocardial infarction (heart attack) includes pain similar to angina which lasts for greater than 30 minutes and does not respond to nitroglycerine. However, 25% of myocardial infarctions are asymptomatic/undetected, i.e. silent myocardial infarctions.

Signs (what the doctor finds on examination)

General examination findings include pallor and anxiety. Examination can be normal, but there may be tachycardia (fast heart rate) hypotension (low BP) and tachypnoea (fast respiratory rate). A low-grade fever (temperature) may be present. There may be a fourth heart sound or evidence of congestive cardiac failure (raised jugular venous pressure, presence of ankle oedema i.e. swollen ankles and bi-basal crepitations). Cardiac murmurs, i.e. mitral incompetence, may become apparent.

Investigations

Electrocardiogram (ECG)

In chronic stable angina the ECG is normal in 33 per cent and may just show minor ischaemic change in many leads.

In a myocardial infarction the ECG will show ST elevation in the relevant leads, with hyperacute T waves. This is followed by the development of Q waves and T-wave inversion. The ECG is normal in 20 per cent of acute myocardial infarctions.

Cardiac enzymes

Enzymes are released from the heart muscle in the presence of a myocardial infarction (heart attack).

Creatinine kinase rises within 6–8 hours of a myocardial infarction, peaks at 24 hours and returns to normal by 2–3 days. A rise can also be due to musculoskeletal damage and in this case the CKMB fraction shows that related to heart muscle alone.

Lactate dehydrogenase rises at 24–48 hours, peaks at 3–5 days and normalises in 7–10 days. AST levels peak at 48–72 hours, but is not specific for myocardial infarction.

Exercise ECG

In patients with chest pain and a normal resting ECG, a standing exercise test is useful in the diagnosis of ischaemic heart disease.

If anginal discomfort occurs during exercise and is associated with > 1 mm ST depression on the ECG, the predictive value for ischaemic heart disease is > 90 per cent.

If a > 2 mm ST depression occurs, this is diagnostic of ischaemic heart disease.

An exercise ECG associated with a significant drop in blood pressure carries an 80 per cent predictive value for ischaemic heart disease.

In patients unable to exercise, a dobutamine ECG/Stress Test can be used.

Magnetic resonance imaging (MRI) has only a limited role in assessing coronary artery disease, although it accurately tells us about ventricular mass and its function.

Management of ischaemic heart disease

Several drugs are available for treatment of angina. These include nitrates, beta-blockers (contra-indicated in patients with asthma and severe heart failure), calcium channel blockers, aspirin and the potassium channel activator Nicorandil.

- Aspirin has been shown to reduce the risk of myocardial infarction by 87 per cent in a 5-year follow-up of men with chronic stable angina and should be given to all patients with no known contraindications.
- Beta-blockers reduce the workload of the heart and improve survival in patients with myocardial infarction and reduce the incidence of reinfarction.
- Nitroglycerine given sublingually is the drug of choice for an acute anginal attack and can be prophylactic if taken prior to exertion. Long-acting oral nitrates are used as secondary therapy.
- If anginal episodes occur during exercise a calcium channel blocker can be beneficial or an ATP-sensitive potassium channel activator.

Patients with unstable angina need inpatient treatment with cardiac monitoring and treatment with aspirin, intravenous heparin and intravenous glycerine trinitrate. Interventional therapy is needed if conservative measures fail. It may be necessary to arrange coronary angiography to assess the severity of the coronary artery stenosis and to see if the patients needs angioplasty or coronary artery bypass graft (CABG) surgery.

Acute myocardial infarction (heart attack)

The cornerstone of management of acute myocardial infarction is prompt emergency care and initial treatment with oxygen, aspirin and diamorphine. Thrombolytic therapy will be discussed in some detail here as it has revolutionised the management of heart attacks, irrespective of age, sex, hypertension, diabetes and previous heart attack. Thrombolytic therapy decreases mortality, improves left ventricular function, decreases the incidence of arrhythmias and improves long-term survival. Thrombolytic therapy accelerates the conversion of plasminogen to plasmin, which dissolves clots. Nearly 80 per cent of thrombosed arteries can be reopened with thrombolytics, but there is a 15-20 per cent reocclusion rate. It is worth remembering that degree of ST segment resolution on ECG is important in evaluating a patient's risk.

Ideally thrombolytic therapy should be given within 6 hours of the onset of the pain, but can be beneficial for up to 12 hours.

Thrombolytic regimes for acute myocardial infarction

Streptokinase	1.5 million units intravenous (i.v.) over 1 hour
tPA Standard iv	10 mg bolus, 50 mg in 1st hour then 40 mg over next 2 hours, followed by i.v. Heparin (5000 u bolus followed by 1000 u/hr)
Accelerated i.v.	10 mg bolus 50 mg over half hour then 40 mg over 1 hour followed by IV Heparin.

Contraindications of thrombolytic treatment

1. Absolute
• Active bleeding from peptic ulcer
• Puncture from a non-compressible vessel
• Aortic dissection
• Active intracranial malignancy
• Recent surgery (< 1 week)
• Pericarditis
• Previous drug allergy (Streptokinase)

2. Relative
• Major trauma/surgery in 6–8 weeks
• Recent cerebrovascular accident (stroke)
• Prolonged CPR (cardiopulmonary resuscitation)
• History of peptic ulceration
• Proliferative diabetic retinopathy
• Severe uncontrolled hypertension

• Pregnancy (although out of context but included for the sake of completeness)
• History of bleeding diatheses
• Cancer
• Severe hepatic dysfunction

Complications of thrombolytic treatment
Allergic reactions to streptokinase (secondary to streptokinase antibodies)
Major bleeding 0.1–0.3 per cent
Haemorrhagic stroke up to 0–6 per cent

Secondary prevention of myocardial infarction (i.e. heart attacks)
Almost half of the patients who die from coronary artery disease are known to have diseased coronary arteries (three-quarters of these deaths occur outside hospital) so there is a strong case for secondary prevention (those who already had heart attacks) of heart attacks. These include drugs, change in life-style and cardiac surgery.

Drugs
1. Aspirin – use has shown reduction in mortality. Dose, usually 75 mgs aspirin daily.
2. Beta-blockers – a 20 per cent reduction in mortality following heart attacks has been shown (this is mainly because of reduction in sudden cardiac deaths) following use of these drugs. If possible the drug should be started after heart attacks. Beta-blockers are, in fact, under-used after heart attacks.
3. ACE Inhibitors – using these drugs following heart attacks is especially useful in patients with evidence of clear cut heart failure but is useful even if function of left ventricle is impaired (i.e. ejection fraction less than 40 per cent).
4. Lipid-lowering drugs – Statins (five Statins are now available Atorvastatin, Cervastatin, Fluvastatin, Pravastatin and Simvastatin)

Significant reduction in mortality is now known to occur following cholesterol-lowering measures (besides it is well known that these drugs are used in primary prevention of coronary artery disease).

Statins may soon become an additional therapeutic consideration in the prevention of cerebro-vascular events, if used after myocardial infarction.

5. Warfarin (an anticoagulant) should be used in patients with atrial fibrillation.

Life-style change

It is a sad fact that many people find it very hard to change their life-style, for example, weight reduction, cigarette smoking and even keeping active and having regular exercise. Nevertheless these are important preventive measures.

Cardiac surgery

Patients should be referred for cardiac investigation such as coronary angiography if there is worsening of symptoms in spite of the use of drugs and life-style changes. (In angiography, contrast medium is injected into coronary arteries after the insertion of cardiac catheters. This is followed by taking views of coronary arteries after repeatedly injecting the dye.)

After the narrowing of coronary arteries has been established, two types of coronary artery surgery may be undertaken.

1. Angioplasty (a balloon is inflated across the narrowing in the coronary artery) There is an increased rate of restenosis and repeated procedures are performed.

2. Coronary artery bypass graft (CABG)

The main consideration as to whether angioplasty or CABG should be performed, depends upon whether there is extensive three-vessel disease of the coronary arteries (here CABG should be preferred) or not, and function of left ventricle.

Ideal time to start preventive measures

As to the vexed question of when should heart disease prevention strategy begin, there is no tailor-made answer. This is because risk factors and people's life-style and behaviour continue all through adulthood and well into the later life. It seems reasonable that the preventive measures, i.e. efforts to correct risk factors, should start early in life. Special attention should be paid to:

1. blood pressure control,
2. stopping smoking,
3. controlling weight and serum cholesterol, and
4. leading an active life.

All chest pains are not due to ischaemic heart disease

Differential diagnosis of chest pain

It is worth remembering that every chest pain is not necessarily due to disease of the coronary artery. Examples include:

1. Anaemia
2. Aortic stenosis
3. Pulmonary embolism
4. Musculo-skeletal pain
5. Oesophageal spasm
6. Peptic ulcer pain and, at times, gall stones

Final message

1. As coronary heart disease is our greatest killer, every effort should be made to prevent and treat this condition.

2. Important preventive measures include meticulous control of hypertension, stopping smoking, control of blood lipids, avoiding obesity and keeping active.

3. Advances in management of coronary artery disease are continuing. Research in heart disease saves life but it is expensive. Help needs to be extended to the British Heart Foundation.

Useful address

British Heart Foundation

14 Fitzhardinge Street,
London W1H 4DH
Tel 0171 935 0185

References/Further reading list

1. *Cardiovascular Disorders*, Part 2 of 5 Vol. 25:11 Medicine International 1997

2. *Cardiac Rehabilitation: Guidelines and Audit Standards* (Eds. David T. Thompson, Gerald S. Bowman, David P. de Bono and Anthony Hopkins). Royal College of Physicians of London, ISBN 186816 048 4

3. *Preventing Coronary Heart Disease: the Role of Antioxidants, Vegetables and Fruit* - (eds. Lesley Rogers and Imogen Sharp). The National Health Forum, HMSO London 1997.

4. *British Journal of Cardiology* Vo..5, May 1998, Page 258.

5. *Lecture Notes in Geriatrics*. (Eds. Nicholas Coni and Stephen Webster) Fifth Edition Blackwell Science, 1998.

6. *Lancet* Vol 35 June 27 1998 issue.

Acknowledgement

I am very grateful to Dr Kate Williamson of The Royal Oldham Hospital for her substantial contribution in preparing this chapter.

Hypertension

CHAPTER 4

Words and Abbreviations used:

BP = blood pressure; hypertension = raised (high) blood pressure, ACE = Angiotensin-converting enzyme, systolic hypertension (where upper level of BP is mainly raised), postural hypotension (marked reduction in blood pressure with change of posture, especially systolic level down by 20 or more), diastolic = lower level of BP

Hypertension is the commonest chronic disorder needing treatment with drugs in the Western World. (1) In Britain, as many as half the men and one-third of the women over 50 years have raised blood pressure. It is a major risk factor for stroke and coronary artery disease. (2)

So what is hypertension?

Hypertension is higher than normal blood pressure. This definition of hypertension then begs two questions.

What is blood pressure? What is its normal value?

Blood pressure is the pressure exerted by the blood on the walls of the arteries. This pressure is dependent upon the efficiency of the heart pump and the calibre and elasticity of the arteries. The blood pressure is not constant. It varies with age – it increases as the age advances. The systolic blood pressure continues to rise for a longer period (into one's 70s) compared to diastolic pressure (into one's 60s). (3) For example, while a blood pressure of 110/70 mm mercury will be normal in a 15 year old, it will be considered to be low for a person say aged 85, whose normal blood pressure will be something like 175/95 (some very old people may well have low blood pressure).

A useful rule of thumb is to add 100 to a person's age in order to know his or her systolic pressure. Of course, there will be individual variations. Apart from age, the pressure may vary from day to day, by time of the day and indeed moment to moment, with exercise, emotion, tobacco, alcohol, meals, bladder distension and pain. Thus, it may spuriously increase by seeing a doctor in his busy surgery or hospital's outpatient department ('white coat hypertension'). It is very important that several readings are taken to establish a base-line level of blood pressure to decide whether treatment is necessary, and also a base-line for monitoring progress.

Role of kidneys

As the kidneys control the two principal determinants of blood pressure (i.e. peripheral resistance and cardiac output), they have a central role in hypertension. The cardiac output is regulated by salt and water balance which in turn modifies the plasma volume while the peripheral resistance is regulated predominantly by renin–antiotensin–aldosterone system. (4)

Types of hypertension

Hypertension is divided as Primary, or Essential, (i.e. no known cause) and Secondary (i.e. cause known). Most elderly patients with hypertension are essential hypertensives (about 95 per cent). Hypertension on its own is largely without symptoms and may herald its presence for the first time as a stroke. It is all the more necessary that the blood pressure should be checked regularly.

Most of the patients with secondary hypertension have longstanding kidney disease. In this context, it is worth mentioning occasional cases of renal artery stenosis which may be unilateral or bilateral. Its importance in elderly patients is due to the fact that in its presence, the use of ACE inhibitors is contraindicated. Coarctation of the aorta causing hypertension is only occasionally found in elderly patients. Hypertension due to endocrine causes in elderly patients is rare. The blood pressure rises slowly in the benign form, but with great rapidity in the malignant (accelerated) form of hypertension. Fortunately, the latter is uncommon in the elderly. The million dollar question has been: *when should hypertension in the elderly be treated?* It is a subject of considerable debate and no doubt it will continue to attract our attention in years to come. Fortunately, since the report by the European Working Party on hypertension in the Elderly (EPHE) we have become wiser on this issue, certainly in treating older hypertensives. Its findings – there was reduction in treated groups of total mortality by 26 per cent, cardiovascular deaths by 27 per cent and cardiovascular events, both fatal and non-fatal, by 36 per cent. These are based on a large number of patients, both men and women into their 70s. It may be that the patients selected for treatment were severely hypertensive, i.e. of high risk groups. It will not be fair to apply the result of this and other trials to hypertensive patients who are 80 years and over. However, further studies have thrown more light on this issue and we have now become wiser (please see HOT Study findings mentioned below).

Borderline hypertension

A fifth of patients with borderline hypertension may be treated unnecessarily. Furthermore, we are probably misdiagnosing and overtreating hypertension. In cases with borderline hypertension, ambulatory blood pressure measurement is the best solution to overcome this problem of overtreating with its attendant undesirable side effects. By this method, the blood pressure measurement is done over time to see what happens. (5)

Who needs treating and what is the upper age limit of patients treated?

It is now generally accepted that by treating hypertension in elderly patients, one can now substantially reduce their cardiovascular complications. (6) It is prudent not to be too dogmatic about the upper age limit, but in general, patients up to the age of 85 need to be treated if the average blood pressure measurement after three readings (say over a 3–6 month period, when efforts should also be made to use non-pharmacological measures, i.e. maintaining optimum body weight, reducing salt intake, avoiding alcohol abuse and where possible, take regular exercise or be more active) is 1.) systolic BP 160 mm mercury or above

2.) diastolic BP is 90 mm mercury or above

However, a recently published Study, i.e. HOT (Hypertension Optimal Treatment) where patients treated were 50–80 years old, shows that (7),

1.) one should aim for BP reduction down to 140/90 or even less, especially in patients with diabetes, where a BP of 140/80 mm mercury should be aimed at.

2.) Aspirin (75 mg) can be recommended when there is evidence of coronary artery disease – provided there is no bleeding risk with the patient.

Treating hypertension soon after an episode of stroke

It is prudent not to lower blood pressure (mild to moderate hypertension) for 10 days or so following acute stroke unless there is evidence of other complications of hypertension, i.e. severe cardiac failure, hypertensive encephalopathy, aortic dissection, or indeed intracerebral haemorrhage.

Drug Treatment of Hypertension (Table)

Drugs used in Treating Hypertension	Comments
1. Thiazide diuretics or Thiazide-like compound	• may have metabolic side effects i.e. gout, hyperglycaemia.
2. Centrally acting drugs such as Methyldopa	• much less in use • postural hypotension is a side effect
3. ACE inhibitors	• well tolerated
Captopril, Enalapril, Lisinopril, Ramipril and others	• may have first dose hypotension as side effect, renal function and plasma potassium level should be monitored.
4. Beta-blockers Atenolol, Celiprolol, Bisoprolol	• contra indicated in cardiac failure and obstructive airways disease • useful

Drugs used in Treating Hypertension	Comments
5. Doxazosin	• postural hypotension and headaches likely side effects.
6. Calcium channel blockers	• useful group
• Verapamil	• generally well tolerated (not used with beta-blockers)
• Nifedipine (retard preparation)	
• Diltiazem	• may cause bradycardia
• Amlodipine, Lacidipine and Felodipine	• long acting, fewer side effects, effective
• Lercanidipine hydrochloride tablet (Zanidip) (recently marketed)	• fewer side effects, also useful in isolated systolic hypertension
7. Angiotensin II receptor antagonists Losartan, Valsartan, Candesartan,	• Do not cause persisent dry cough (so useful if ACE inhibitors cannot be used)
Irbesartan	• monitor plasma potassium

Note: Drug combinations

Combinations of the above drugs are used only after failure from using optimal dose of single agents to control hypertension. There is not much to be gained by combining beta-blockers and ACE inhibitors or the Sartans (i.e. angiotensin II receptor antagonists) and so also thiazide diuretics and calcium channel blockers. Other drug combinations, especially thiazide diuretics and beta-blockers, are effective.

Summary of overall management of hypertension

1. *Correct diagnosis of hypertension*

It is very important that the diagnosis of hypertension be made correctly. For this, right techniques should be used to measure blood pressure. These include proper cuff applications and reading of the pressure. The systolic pressure is recorded when the sound appears (Phase 1) and the diastolic pressure as the sound disappears (Phase 5). Blood pressure measurement with technically simple electronic sphygmomanometer is more accurate. Ambulatory blood pressure monitoring should be considered in managing borderline, difficult, or 'office' (white coat) hypertension. Considering all the pros and cons, this should be cost effective. All in all, when so much is at stake on level of blood pressure, it is vital that blood pressure is measured correctly.

2. *Full assessment of the patient*

A complete clinical evaluation of the patient, including a careful history (of smoking, excessive alcohol intake and kidney disease, family history of ischaemic heart disease or stroke) should be taken. The base line investigations include urine examination for protein, glucose and culture and sensitivity; full blood count; blood urea, creatinine, uric acid and electrolyte estimation, an ECG and a chest X-ray (to show evidence of cardiac enlargement). Specialist investigations (abdominal ultrasound, echocardiogram, arteriography and renin studies) will be needed only in selected cases and quite infrequently. Every patient should have his weight taken. In general, the chances of operative interference to cure hypertension in the elderly are very small indeed.

3. *Is drug treatment needed?*

It is important to ask oneself as to whether the patient needs drug treatment, especially if the patient is over 85 and has a mild hypertension with no evidence of target-organ dysfunction, i.e. cardiomegaly (i.e. enlarged heart) with or without cardiac failure, kidney failure and retinopathy. In this situation non-pharmacological measures should be tried which have been found to be of benefit. The measures include low salt diet, cutting down alcohol consumption, regular exercise, reduction in weight and stopping cigarette smoking.

4. *Is there a secondary cause?*

Ruling out the cause of hypertension by appropriate tests will be needed in very few cases. Uncommon conditions, like renal artery stenosis and coarctation of aorta, are found in less than 1 per cent of elderly patients.

5. *Prescribe correct medication – drug therapy should be individualised*

In the past a conventional stepped triple therapy (a thiazide diuretic, a beta-blocker and if necessary, a vasodilator) approach has been used. However, patients are now prescribed drugs which are in keeping with their overall medical condition. For example, beta-blockers should not be prescribed in chronic obstructive airways disease, and peripheral vascular disease. Methyldopa should certainly be avoided in patients with depression and liver dysfunction. It is prudent to avoid thiazide diuretic in diabetic patients in view of their metabolic effects. ACE inhibitors are now well established in treatment of all grades of hypertension and they are now more suitable than other hypotensives for the treatment of hypertension in diabetics. ACE inhibitors can be used with calcium antagonists. One must however, be aware of a few occasional problems associated with the use of ACE inhibitors:

- Marked symptomatic hypotension after the first dose, especially in those already on high doses of diuretics.
- Hyperkalaemia if used in conjunction with potassium conserving diuretics.
- Chronic dry cough which may be persistent.

Calcium antagonists have been widely used in hypertension either singly or in combination with other drugs. Their side effects are comparatively minimal. Their hypotensive effect correlates directly with age and inversely with plasma renin activity. Elderly hypertensives with associated angina particularly benefit from this group of drugs. (8)

As left ventricular hypertrophy is an important risk factor, it is helpful to remember that beta-blockers (e.g. Atenolol), ACE inhibitors (e.g. Captopril) and thiazide diuretic (hydrochlorthiazide) significantly reduce left ventricular mass in men with mild to moderate hypertension (9)

6. *Ethnic background and response of BP lowering drugs.*

Afro-caribbean patients may have reduced response to ACE inhibitors and to beta-blockers. Calcium channel blockers are effective in such patients.

7. *Blood pressure should be lowered slowly*

When a decision to treat hypertension has been made, the blood pressure should be brought down slowly. Sudden reduction in pressure may precipitate a stroke, one of the events one is trying to prevent. The important issue of whether to treat isolated systolic hypertension (ISH) is now settled, i.e. benefit was noted from treating ISH in trial of elderly patients.

8. *Consider other coronary risk factors*

While a patient's hypertension is being treated, efforts should be made to take into account all the other risk factors for coronary heart disease, like cigarette smoking, high serum cholesterol and diabetes. After all, coronary artery disease is our greatest enemy.

9. *Compliance*

One should always check if patients are taking prescribed drugs regularly. For this to happen, the drug doses should be simplified, say, prescribed in at least twice daily doses. Drug doses and indeed the necessity to continue medication must be explained to the patients from time to time when they attend the surgery/outpatient clinic.

10. *Reduce alcohol consumption (two to three units daily at most)*

It is now considered important to advise patients to reduce alcohol consumption, as a means of lowering their blood pressure.

11. *Quality of life – the eleventh commandment*

Patient's quality of life should not be compromised by overtreating high blood pressure with side effects like postural hypotension and falls – no one should bear worse side effects from drugs than disease itself.

Final message

1. There is significant reduction in morbidity and mortality by blood pressure reduction in patients with combined systolic/diastolic or only systolic hypertension.

2. We should be aware of the immense task – about 10 per cent of patients aged between 10 and 79 years have hypertension.

3. Sadly, the 'Rule of Halves' described in the 1970s still applies – it is that half of those detected hypertensive are not treated and half of those treated are uncontrolled. So, every effort should be made to detect more and more cases of hypertension in the community. There is thus a case for advocating more 'Hypertension Clinics' in the General Practitioner's surgeries. Indeed, blood pressure of all patients visiting their General Practitioner should be recorded. Happily these days, we do not see many cases of hypertension needing emergency treatment. This must be due to effective treatment of less severe cases of hypertension and the decline of some forms of renal disease.

4. A diuretic or beta-blocker is still the best drug for starting the treatment of hypertension provided there are no contra-indications. If necessary they may be combined.

5. Clinical trials are needed to determine if mild differences in therapeutic benefits of anti-hyper-

tensive drugs, i.e. their ability to alter metabolic profiles (for example, lipid levels or insulin glu-cose relations) or to reverse left ventricular hypertrophy are clinically significant.(10)

Useful address

British Hypertension Society
127 High Street,
Teddington,
Middlesex TW11 8HH
Tel: 0181 977 0012; Fax 0181 977 0055

References

1. Summary of recent advances in treatment of hypertension, in *ABC of Hypertension*, 1987, 40–42. British Medical Journal, London.

2. A – Z of Preventive Medicine, Part One, *Sunday Times* (1989)

3. 'Cardiovascular disease', in Coni, N., Davison, W. and Webster, S., *Lecture Notes in Geriatrics*, Blackwell Science, 5th Edn. 1998.

4. 'Renal hypertension'. Main, J., in Catto, G.R.D. and Power, D.A. (eds), *Nephrology in Clinical Practice*, 1988, 236–53. Edward Arnold, London.

5. Editorial, *British Medical Journal*, 1988, p 297.

6. *British National Formulary* No. 35 (March 1998) - A joint publications of British Medical Association and the Royal Pharmaceutical Society of Great Britain.

7. Blood pressure targets: the lower the better? by Graham Jackson in *Update for General Practitioners*, 24 June 1998 issue

8. Sloan, R.W., 'Alternative first line therapies in geriatric hypertension', *Geriatrics*, 1989, 44: 61–72.

9. *Lancet* May 3, 1997 issue (science and medicine section)

10. Pfeffer, M.A., and Pfeffer, J.M., 'Reversing cardiac hypertrophy in hypertension', *The New England Journal of Medicine*, 1990, 322: 1388–89.

Further Reading List

1. *Clinical Atlas of Hypertension* by John D. Swales, Peter S. Sever and Sir Stanley Peart, Gower Medical Publishing 1991.

2. *Hypertension in Practice* (D.G. Beevers and B.A. MacGregor) 2nd Edition Dunitz, London 1995.

3. *Blood Pressure Measurement* E.T. O'Brian, J.C. Petrie, W.A. Littler, M. de Swiet, P.L. Padfield, M.J. Dillon, A. Coats and F. Mee: 3rd Edition (1997)

Management of Diabetes

CHAPTER 5

Diabetes mellitus is one of the most common among chronic diseases. It is estimated that world-wide there are over 100 million diabetic patients and that 5.8 per cent of total health care in Europe is spent on treating such patients. So what is diabetes? It is characterised by passing excessive amount of glucose-containing urine, with thirst and general malaise. This is caused by failure of β cells in the pancreas to produce sufficient insulin.

As insulin is necessary to convert the glucose (a sugar which is part of carbohydrate food) to energy, the resultant effect is an excessive accumulation of glucose in the blood. The diagnosis of diabetes is confirmed if the random glucose is 11 mmol/l or more.

Diabetes exists in at least 2 per cent of the elderly population, the majority of whom have type II diabetes mellitus. This is also called non-insulin-dependent diabetes.

A small proportion of elderly patients have type I, or insulin-dependent diabetes. This minority group have either developed this condition in old age or have survived with this condition.

Diabetes may be associated with diseases of the pancreas, diseases with hormonal disorders and taking of drugs, such as steroids.

In this chapter I will highlight the main problems in the management of diabetes and thus would emphasise the value of education, and would plead for the setting up of more General Practitioner (GP)-run diabetic clinics (mini-clinics) in the community.

Presentation of diabetes

In many patients diabetes is a chance finding. In others it may be present with many of its complications such as failing vision (due to diabetic retinopathy), heart attack (it is a major contributor to the development of cardiovascular disease), gangrene or sepsis of the feet, or even diabetic coma.

A diabetic patient is also frequently subject to other illnesses and these include hypertension, stroke, infection of the skin (e.g. carbuncle) and kidneys.

Management of diabetes

The important factor in the development of type II diabetes is obesity. Most elderly patients do not need insulin. Their diabetes is controlled by dietary restriction or by a combination of dietary restriction and oral drugs.

The diet should contain adequate carbohydrates with high fibres. Eating fresh fruits, salads and vegetables should be encouraged. The fat in the diet should be reduced by restriction on fried food, cream and butter. (A useful diabetic cookery book is *Cooking for Diabetics* by Jill Metcalfe, Published by Thorsons.)

In an elderly patient, the control of diabetes should be flexible, easy to follow and without the hazards of possible hypoglycaemia (low blood sugar). One should take into account his or her other diseases and hence other medications. Thus the possibility of drug interactions should be kept in mind. Diabetes is an important risk factor in atherosclerosis (hardening of the arteries).

It is now generally agreed that in many patients, diabetic eye complications (retinopathy), kidney failure, strokes and ischaemic foot problems (say, gangrene) may be prevented by adequate management of diabetes.

Mini-clinics

It is essential therefore, that diabetics are seen in organised clinics, both in hospital and in the community. No doubt geriatricians should be involved in seeing elderly diabetics in special diabetic clinics, but elderly diabetics can benefit by attending GP diabetic clinics (mini-clinics) too.

These clinics may be started by young, enthusiastic and interested GPs. Patients find that in these clinics there is continuity of care and they do not have to wait. Many patients may prefer the small, friendly GP diabetic clinic environment to a large, impersonal hospital outpatient/diabetic clinic. (Many patients do not attend hospital diabetic clinics as they have to wait for a long time, consultation time is short and they probably see a new doctor each time and hence are not altogether satisfied.)

My plea, therefore, is that enthusiastic GPs should be given encouragement for starting diabetic mini-clinics in the community.

Of course, close liaison between hospital diabetes clinics and these mini-clinics should be maintained. GPs will need help from hospital doctors, such as geriatricians, general physicians, biochemists and ophthalmic and vascular surgeons. This should include regular meetings and case presentations concerning both aspects of diabetic care, i.e. prevention as well as treatment of diabetic complications. Diabetes is a good example of shared care.

Services available

It is essential that diabetic patients should benefit from the wide range of special services which are needed for the overall management of diabetes.

These services are:
1. A foot service from a chiropodist.
2. An eye service from an ophthalmologist – patient's eyes must be seen at least once a year.
3. A dietetic service from a dietician.
4. The services of a vascular surgeon may be required.
5. Educational services – besides treatment, the physician provides education to diabetic patients, but this can ideally be given by a diabetes specialist nurse or health visitor.

Education on simple foot hygeine, proper footwear, avoidance of damaging extremes of heat and cold and regular attention by a chiropodist are 'musts' for all diabetic patients. *It has rightly been said that diabetics should keep their feet as clean as their mouths.* This is mainly to prevent any infection or ulceration. After all, most amputations in a diabetic patient usually start with an ulcer. (It is estimated that £13 million is spent on amputation alone in the United Kingdom.) (1)

As obesity is a very important factor in the development of diabetes in later life (type II diabetes), weight reduction can reduce or even reverse the diabetic process along with problems like hypertension and abnormal blood lipid levels. Besides, all patients must have a working knowledge of diabetes, of its major complications, including complications of treatment, such as hypoglycaemia.

Prevention of complications

To avoid vascular diseases, diabetic patients should be advised to take more exercise, stop smoking and eat less animal fat. The long-term benefits of these preventive measures are clearly immense. So, the supervision of control of diabetes, a close watch on the probable complications of diabetes and education in prevention of complications are the main components of comprehensive diabetic care.

Management of diabetes

Treatment of diabetes mellitus (type II or maturity onset diabetes). The three aims are:
1. To keep raised blood sugar reasonably under control and patients feeling of well-being.
2. To avoid hypoglycaemia. This can be especially harmful to those who drive a car (see below).
3. Hopefully to prevent diabetic complications.

   Three options are available for blood sugar control:
1.) Diet (if a person is overweight, weight reducing diet to be given) but in general, diet should have less fat and carbohydrate refined of the high-fibre variety.
2.) Oral drugs: three groups
a.) Sulphonylureas group of drugs: Tolbutamide, Gliclazide, Glipizide and the newly marketed Glimepiride.
b.) Biguanides: Metformin, helpful in patients who are overweight.
c.) Others: Acarbose, can also be prescribed when above mentioned drugs do not control the blood sugar.
3) Insulin: one should not hesitate to prescribe insulin in elderly patients, if it is needed – if the diabetes is not controlled by a combination of dietary and oral drugs. It is given by subcutaneous injection, once or twice daily. Insulin can be given by 'Pens' (insulin is in a cartridge and the pen meters the necessary dose).

'Hypos'

Every diabetic should understand the implication of 'hypos' (hypoglycaemia). Here the blood sugar is less than normal. The patient develops mental confusion, bizarre behaviour and ultimately lapses into a coma. It is a most common complication of insulin therapy but is found even if patients are on oral antidiabetic drugs. What can be done about it? There are several preventive measures. Every diabetic patient must be told about this complication. He or she should carry some sugar cubes, biscuits, or any sugar-containing beverage in case it is needed.

In mild cases – when the patient is able to swallow – these are sufficient to reverse the symptoms of hypoglycaemia, but if the patient is drowsy or unconscious, glucose intravenously or 1 mg of Glucagon intramuscularly should be given as soon as possible.

Furthermore, every diabetic patient must carry a card or an identification bracelet bearing his or her and physician's names and telephone numbers. The card must show that the patient is diabetic and in the event of being found unconscious, should be taken to a hospital by ambulance immediately.

British Diabetic Associations (BDA)

The BDA provides a welfare advisory service. It produces publications in the form of dietary recommendations, fact sheets, etc. Members receive a free copy of their bi-monthly journal *Balance*.

The BDA also organises educational holidays for children and adults, and is the greatest single funder of research in the various aspects of diabetes (please see address of BDA at the end of this chapter).

Advances in management

Several developments have taken place in the management of diabetes:

Type I Diabetes

1. Continuous subcutaneous infusion of insulin via a battery-operated portable pump. This may well be the best hope of preventing the eye and kidney complications.
2. Research is also taking place on ways to improve the absorption of insulin from nasal sprays.
3. Pancreatic transplantation in diabetes is another development. Though well over 1000 operations had been done until 1993, there are unfortunately problems associated with this operation, including that of immunosuppression.

Type II Diabetes

Both the *British Medical Journal* and *Lancet* (in their issues of 12 September 1998) carried important messages concerning the management of Type II diabetes, based on the findings of UK Prospective Diabetes Study Group. The messages could be summarised as follows:

1. Obesity and inactivity are mainly responsible for the development of Type II diabetes.
2. Tightly controlled blood glucose concentration reduces the risk of complications in Type II diabetes.
3. Sulphonylureas and insulin produce equal benefit and Metformin also works.
4. In patients with hypertension and Type II diabetes, tight control of blood pressure resulted in 24 per cent reduction in any diabetic complication and 32 per cent reduction in death related to diabetes, i.e. mostly from heart attacks and strokes, Captopril and Atenolol were equally effective in reducing blood pressure and progression of retinopathy. Clearly tight control of blood pressure reduces diabetic complications, also tight control of blood pressure is cost effective.

Summary of management

1. A meticulous control of diabetes in younger age groups and a flexible approach in the elderly should be aimed at.
2. In all diabetics, education should be the main theme and should reflect the motto of the World Health Organisation:

   'If we treat you we help you today, if we teach you, we help you for your life time'.

   This could ideally be provided by a Diabetic Specialist Nurse.
3. If overweight, patients should be asked to lose weight.
4. Patients should be assessed yearly for diabetic eye complications, especially retinopathy.
5. Foot care – care of feet/foot infections or ulcers should be managed with urgency. Patients should have suitable well-fitting footwear.
6. Patients should be told about hypoglycaemia and how to prevent it.
7. A multidisciplinary team approach in the management of diabetes should be the aim.
8. Smoking and other risk factors for ischaemic heart disease (abnormal lipids, hypertension) should be treated. Cardiovascular disease is the main risk in Type II diabetes.
9. Patients should ideally carry a card (showing diabetic medications – insulin or oral medications – name of GP/Consultant).
10. Shared care with hospital diabetic services should be aimed at.

Final message

Diabetes is one disease where the patients have to be their own doctor, i.e. to follow a treatment regime and diet, keep an eye on blood sugar control and diabetic complications and demand a high degree of care from all professionals looking after them. (2)

Useful address

The British Diabetic Association
10 Queen Anne Street,
London W1M OBD
Tel: 0171 323 1531

References

1. *British Medical Journal* Vol 317 (8 August, 1998 issue) (A report by DECOEDE Study Group on behalf of the European Diabetes Epidemiology Study Group.

2. Advanced wound healing and the diabetic foot. (a conference report London UK – 30 October 1997) reported in *Practical Diabetes International* March/April 1998, Vol. 15 (pages i – iii).

3. *A Guide to Care of the Elderly* (Eds. R.B.Shukla and D. Brooks) – Chapter on Diabetes Mellitus by T. L. Dornan – 1996, H.M.S.O. Books

Further reading list

1. *Diabetes and Endocrinology in Clinical Practice* (W. Michael Turnbridge and Phillip D. Home), 1991; Edward Arnold.

2. *Clinics in Geriatric Medicine*, November, 1990, W.B. Saunders, Philadelphia, London.

3. *Endocrinology and Metabolic Clinics of North America* (current Therapies for Diabetes Issue) September, 1997; W.B. Saunders Co., Philadelphia, London.

4. *A Guide to the Guidelines. Disease Management Made Simple*, 3rd edition. (Ed. Peter Smith), Radcliffe Medical Press. 1997 £16.50 ISBN 185775 286 4.

5. *ABC of Diabetes*, 4th Edition. Peter J. Watkins. BMJ Publishing Group 1998 (£14.95) ISBN 07279 1189 9

Did you know?

- It costs at least £200,000 to train a doctor – there is already a shortage of 1,000 GPs and 8,000 nurses.

- While the average length of stay in hospital was 45 days in the 1950s, now it is 8 days.
  The answer to the funding problem is either a mix of public and private money **or** a tax rise.
  Despite its manifold failings, the NHS is the best Health Service in the world.
  [Source: *The Times*, June 23 1998]

Management of Stroke

CHAPTER 6

Management of stroke has been discussed here with special emphasis given on early diagnosis, treatment and rehabilitation. The changing role of Day Hospitals has also been discussed. The chapter ends with a useful reading list, including a list of helpful booklets for the use of patients with stroke and their relatives.

Stroke is the third commonest cause of death after heart attack and cancer in the Western World. Indeed, 90% of all strokes occur in people over the age of 65 years. It is also the most important cause of disability with patients needing considerable after-care. As many people do not understand what stroke means – this may clearly delay diagnosis and vital early treatment in many patients – it should in fact be called 'brain attack' like its heart counterpart, the 'heart attack'.

So what is stroke then?

Stroke is sudden, focal, neurological deficit, mainly due to cerebral infarction or haemorrage with symptoms lasting more than 24 hours. It is also called cerebrovascular accident (transient ischaemic attack (TIA) or mini-stroke is the name given to such an event if lasting up to 24 hours). Considerable progress has been made both in the investigation and management of stroke in specialised Stroke Units. These include imaging of blood vessels, the brain and the heart, treatment of cerebral thrombosis with thrombolytics and rehabilitation of stroke patients with a dedicated multi disciplinary team.

At this stage it will be helpful to explain some words and abbreviations which are commonly used in stroke-related meetings and conferences and many of these are used in this article. This further emphasises the stroke-related research globally and the increasing importance of this condition.

Word and abbreviations explained

Words

• Transient ischaemic attacks (i.e. TIAs also called mini-strokes). These usually do not cause fainting or loss of consciousness. There may, however, be brief episodes of confusion, headache, pins and needles, slurring of speech and weakness. The patient is back to normal well within 24 hours.

- Diplopia – double vision.
- Carotid ultrasound – also called Doppler scan. In this procedure, sound waves are used to take pictures of blood vessels in the neck to find narrowing of artery.
- Artery – a blood vessel carrying oxygen-rich blood to various parts of the body.
- Angiogram – is a special X-ray. First, the patient is given a local anaesthetic. A fine tube introduced through the artery of the groin, is advanced into the artery carrying blood into the brain. X-rays are then taken after injecting a special dye into the vessels. This procedure is undertaken in order to find any narrowing of *the artery in the neck of the brain.*
- Thrombolysis – is dissolving the blood-clots by injection of drugs. In suitable patients with acute strokes this is proving to be very helpful, if given early. (Currently being practised mainly in the USA and continental Europe.)
- Carotid endarterectomy – in order to reduce the risk of strokes, this operation removes a narrowing from carotid artery in the neck.
- Stroke units – these specialist units are based in many District General Hospitals from where stroke teams manage patients who have suffered acute stroke. Apart from doctors, the stroke team consists of nurses, physiotherapists, occupational therapists, speech and language therapists, dietitians, social workers and, sometimes, a clinical psychologist. A close liaison with a neurologist, a vascular surgeon, a neurosurgeon and a cardiologist is essential for overall management of stroke patients.
- Meta-analysis – a conclusion based on results of several studies/researches on the same topic.

Abbreviations

AF = Atrial fibrillation
CVA = Cerebrovascular accident
CAVATAS = Carotid and vertebral artery transluminal angioplasty study

IS = Ischaemic stroke – (commonest cause of stroke)
IST = International stroke trial
FIS = First ever ischaemic stroke
ASPS = Austrian stroke prevention study
TCD = Transcranial Doppler sonography
SAH = Subarachnoid haemorrhage
CT Brain Scan = Computerised tomography brain scan
MRI = Magnetic resonance imaging
MCA = Middle cerebral artery
PET = Positron emission tomography
EBM = Evidence-based medicine
NOM = Neuro-ophthalmic manifestations
IV = Intravenous
ICA = Internal carotid artery
TT = Thrombolytic therapy
EUSI = European stroke initiative
ASA = Acetylsalicylic acid (Aspirin)
CAST = Chinese acute stroke trial
TPA = Tissue plasminogen activator
MI = Myocardial infarction
ACST = Asymptomatic carotid surgery trial
PVD = Peripheral vascular disease
ESPS -2 = Second European stroke prevention study
MB = Micro-bleed
CAPRIE = Aspirin in patients at risk of ischaemic events
CH&S = Chest, heart and stroke (A medical charity which operates in Scotland and Wales)
ADL = Activities of daily living
VSS = Volunteer stroke service

Size of the problem

Every year, 700,000 Europeans are hospitalised or die following a stroke. On average, about a quarter of stroke patients die within a month and about half within 6 months. Stroke imposes a considerable burden on the health-care system both for treating acute cases and for rehabilitation and after-care. This is likely to increase further as people are living longer than ever before. Clearly, effective therapies are urgently needed to improve both mortality and morbidity following this devastating illness.

It is worth emphasising that not all stroke patients have loss of consciousness and complete paralysis of one half of the body. The severity of the symptoms and signs vary – patients may be fully conscious with mild weakness of the arm and/or leg without difficulty of speech or swallowing. These patients clearly do not need specialised treatment as discussed below.

Management of acute stroke

To provide crucial necessary treatment during the early hours of the cerebral dysfunction, it is vitally important for the doctor to make not only an accurate but a rapid diagnosis too of acute stroke (many medical conditions appear similar to stroke, such as brain tumour, epilepsy, hypoglycaemia, multiple sclerosis in younger patients, migraine and many others.) Usually, TIA or even a fully fledged stroke is not confused with the above conditions if a careful history of the event is taken, progress followed and investigations – both routine and special, including CT Brain Scan (even NMR, if indicated) – performed.

There are two major types of strokes:
1. Ischaemic – this is the major type and is due to narrowing and/or blocking of an artery supplying the brain.
2. Haemorrhagic type – due to rupture of arterial walls.

Until now acute stroke management has been largely supportive (e.g. nursing care, maintenance of fluid and electrolytes – balance and nutritional care). This is necessary anyway. However, there has been an advance in recent years with the introduction of thrombolytic therapy (currently being practiced mainly in the USA and continental Europe). Speed is of the essence. To start with, management should include full clinical evaluation of the patient (including evaluation of vital functions). Investigations include blood tests, ECG, CT brain scan and where necessary, echocardiogram or angiography. Magnetic resonance imaging is needed in special circumstances. These measures are undertaken to arrive at the correct diagnosis and treatment of complicating factors like anoxia, raised intracranial pressure, cardiac arrhythmias, high blood pressure, seizures, raised temperature, as they clearly influence the brain injury brought about by ischaemic insult.

Treatment of acute stroke includes both restoring blood flow in the brain and providing neuroprotection. These jobs are well done by thrombolysis – it re-opens occluded blood vessels and increases cerebral blood supply. Trials have shown that to have a beneficial effect, intravenous therapy with t-PA, should be given within 3 hours in selected stroke patients to salvage viable neurons surrounding the core infarct. (In spite of possible side effect such as intra-cranial haemorrhage; thrombolysis, nevertheless, should be considered in selected patients with ischaemic stroke).

Patients treated with t-PA have shown improved overall performance including that in ADL. The success of thrombolytic therapy has led to renewed interest in its use for ischaemic stroke. Thrombolytic therapy in acute ischaemic stroke was the main theme in the May, 1998 European Stroke Conference in Edinburgh, UK.

Rehabilitation of stroke patients and stroke units

Rehabilitation is the restoration of a patient's physical, mental, or social disability to its fullest functioning state. The main aim of rehabilitation, therefore, is to reduce the disabling effect of stroke. The success of rehabilitation depends on a wide number of factors, which can be physical – (following stroke or arthritis), mental (confusion and depression) or social (living alone, recently bereaved or under-nourished) conditions. Disablements fall into three categories: impairment (deficiency in the body), disability (affecting everyday living activities), and handicap (social disadvantage and dependency). Multiple risk factors should always be looked for and managed.

One in five medical admissions are down to neurological conditions.

Organised stroke unit care has resulted in long-term reductions in death, dependency and the need for institutional care.

The benefits are not restricted to any particular group of patients, and there has been no systematic increase in length of stay.

Multidisciplinary care, apart from consultant in charge, is from a G-grade sister and other nursing staff, physiotherapist, occupational therapist, speech therapist and occasionally a clinical psychologist, with preferably a centre-manager to co-ordinate care.

There is a clear-cut protocol regarding admission policy, discharge and transfer policy and aftercare, while liaison with social services is maintained at all times.

Nutrition

In order to have full benefit from rehabilitation, patients should have adequate nutrition. Those particularly frail, forgetful, postoperative and malnourished should be assessed by a dietitian and be given the necessary nutrients.

A patient with malnutrition will need a much longer rehabilitation time, and may not benefit as much as expected.

Discharge arrangements

It is vital that GPs and other necessary agencies such as social services and district nurses are promptly informed of the patient's details, such as diagnosis, progress, medications, follow-up, time and destination of discharge and support services.

Preventive measures (stroke and related conditions)

Prevention is better than cure. During the period of rehabilitation in hospital, certain preventive measures should be undertaken by relevant members of the multi-disciplinary care team. They are:

1. Advice, such as suitable posture, especially while sitting, of a patient with back pain. Patients who had a fall at home should be taught how to get up and summon help if they fall again. This is especially important for frail elderly people.

2. Full assessment of drugs, especially:
   a. those likely to cause postural hypotension (marked BP reduction on posture change) such as sleeping tablets;
   b. other psychotropic drugs, including tranquillisers, anti-depressants and antipsychotics;
   c. diuretics (water tablets).

3. Advice regarding regular walking should be given to patients with osteoporosis and back pain due to collapsed vertebrae (bones of the spine). This will improve balance and reduce the risk of falling and thus of bone fractures.

4. Preventive measures for recurrence of stroke, including:
   a. life-style changes such as exercise, stopping smoking (a risk factor to cause stroke in its own right) and eating a low-fat diet;
   b. drugs to control diabetes and hypertension ; if there is no haemorrhage, Aspirin, (although not prescribed in those with active peptic ulcer, very confused or who have side effects due to aspirin) Dipyridamole, Clopidogrel or anti-coagulants (drugs such as Warfarin, used against dangerous clots formed in blood vessels);
   c. consider surgery on arteries of the neck in patients who are fit and below the age of 85; (on current indications, arterial blockage

should be 70 per cent or more, to be considered for surgery).

Achieving success

The success of a rehabilitation programme in a Stroke Unit setting depends upon the following factors:

1. Enthusiam and professionalism of all concerned and multidisciplinary team approach.
2. Picking the right patient for rehabilitation. (Patients with multiple pathologies including confusional states clearly do not do well.)
3. Adequate staffing.
4. Co-ordinated care through regular team meetings.
5. Participation of carers/family in the rehabilitation process.
6. Training and education programme for staff.
7. Research and regular audit.

Patient's satisfaction versus 'out-put'

The satisfaction of patients and their improved quality of life should be given due consideration when evaluating services.

In a *British Medical Journal* article (October 25 1997), it was suggested that for early discharge of patients with stroke, community rehabilitation is feasible and is as effective as conventional hospital care. It is also acceptable to patients, and it considerably cuts the use of hospital beds. The article states *"an opportunity may exist to shift resources from hospital to community care for this common and expensive condition"*. Indeed, we need more integration between hospital-based medical care and care in the community, with the barrier between the two services removed. This is the way forward to provide adequate, more acceptable and cost-effective services to elderly patients in the 21st century.

The Audit Commission Report 'Coming of Age' (October 1997) is very much welcomed as, among other things, it clearly sets out joint working between health and social services. (Please see chapter 20 on Community Care)

Day hospitals and stroke rehabilitation

Traditionally day hospitals up and down the country have been used, along with wards and patient's homes, for rehabilitation of patients with stroke. Lately the functioning of the day hospitals has come under severe criticism from several researches and audits.

So what has gone wrong?

The reasons for change include poor attendance by patients – indeed many day hospitals have now closed. There are also differing service expectations by the patients and their relatives on one hand and the members of the multidisciplinary team on the other.

The absence of nationally accepted guidelines has complicated the matter further. We now work in an environment where evidence-based medicine and rehabilitation, audit and outcome measures and cost-effectiveness are becoming the order of the day. (In principle, there is nothing wrong with these, but we should not forget the one very important ingredient of overall patient care, which is patient satisfaction.)

The effect of all this is that day hospitals have been developed to provide a wide variety of patient activities. They range from Specialist Clinics such as those for Parkinson's disease, osteoporosis and memory clinic, to endoscopy and blood transfusion. It can thus be seen that the functioning of the traditional day hospital has changed rapidly.

So what are the possible solutions for the functioning of day hospitals in the next millennium?

We all know that existing institutions are currently in a state of evolution and day hospitals are no exception. There are several possible solutions to the current confusion surrounding the functioning of day hospitals. They are:

1. Day hospitals should be easily accessible to GPs.

For this to happen, hospitals' admission departments, accident and emergency units and day hospitals should work in co-ordination and not function independently.

2. It is said that there is too much waiting by patients and comparatively little time spent on rehabilitation. The situation could be improved by:

a. An improvement in transport arrangements;

b. As stroke patients form the largest group needing rehabilitation, thought should be given to being treated in their own homes, or even at day centres;

c. The involvement of the private sector to help fund more day hospital places.

One suggestion is that the private sector could help provide rehabilitation facilities in the community, which would take away the pressure from hospitals where parking is a major problem.

This could cause problems, however, through lack of specialist supervision and for carrying out investigative procedures in the community.

Multiple pathologies and other related problems in elderly patients leave a large grey area in research and outcomes. We have to ask the right questions to get the right answers, so perhaps we need to be more selective in analysing the outcomes. All in all, the functioning of day hospitals is currently in a state of flux, and we do not yet know if they will disappear like dinosaurs or rise from the ashes like a phoenix. Time alone will tell.

Management of stroke in the 21st century

Over 2,500 years after this condition was first recorded, the management of this condition is now approaching a very critical and exciting stage as we enter the 21st century. Besides providing primary prevention, our job is to diagnose the acute strokes quickly and accurately and (a) provide acute care ideally in Stroke Units and (b) provide secondary prevention and (c) arrange comprehensive rehabilitation, where needed.

Every District General Hospital should have a well functioning Specialist Stroke Unit so that people suffering from stroke – mostly elderly patients – do not lose out. Goldring in *The Age of Rationing*, an excellent television programme on Channel 4 TV (June 28, 1998), made this point exceedingly well.

Final message

1. There is now an opportunity for treating an acute stroke (i.e. ischaemic strokes), where damaged neurons may be salvaged by thrombolytic therapy in carefully selected patients. We in this country should not lag behind.

2. Stroke rehabilitation is an important component of overall stroke management. There is now also a need for extending stroke rehabilitation in the community.

3. Efforts to prevent stroke (treatment of hypertension, using antiplatelet agents, carotid artery surgery, which is currently underperformed) must continue.

4. Social and emotional needs of stroke patient should receive due attention.

5. There have been suggestions of creating stroke medicine as a separate subspecialty. This needs due consideration.

Useful addresses

1. **British Brain and Spine Foundation**
   7 Winchester House,
   Cranmer Road,
   London SW9 6EJ

2. **The Stroke Association**
   Stroke House,
   Whitecross Street,
   London EC1Y 8JJ
   Tel 0171 490 7999
   Fax 0171 490 2686

(The information centres – all over the country – are staffed by trained organisers and volunteers).

References and further reading list

1. *Advances in Acute Stroke Management – information and abstracts* (a satellite symposium at the 7th Stroke Conference in Edinburgh 28 May 1998.

2. *Measurement in Neurological Rehabilitation – E.U.S.I.* by Dr. D. T. Wade. Oxford Publications, 1992

3. *Future Strategy for the N.H.S. – A Position Paper –* British Medical Association – London.

4. *Stroke – A Practical Guide to Management* by C.P. Warlow and others, Blackwell Science Ltd. 1996 (An excellent detailed text on stroke).

5. *Geriatric Day Hospitals – Their Roles and Guidelines for Good Practice.* The Royal College of Physicians, February 1994.

Booklets

1. *Stroke – questions and answers* (available from The Stroke Association) (address as above).

2. *What is carotid endartertomy* (by Charles Warlow) available from The Stroke Association.

3. *Speech, Language and Communication Difficulties – A Guide for patients and Carers,* available from British Brain and Spine Foundation (address as above).

4. *Transient Ischaemic Attacks and/or Mild Strokes* (available from British Brain and Spine Foundation).

5. *Keeping Well after your Stroke.* The Stroke Association, 1997

Arthritis and Back Pain

CHAPTER 7

Arthritis and back pain are common causes of disability in the elderly population. The disability is made worse by several other factors including co-existence of other medical problems, psychosocial aspects of chronic disorders and not to mention the changes due to normal ageing. In this chapter the main emphasis will be on osteoarthritis: – commonest form of arthritis in the elderly population – and back pain. Although back pain is most prevalent among people in their middle years, many people continue to have the problem in later years. Finally, the chapter concludes with a brief mention of rheumatoid arthritis and acute arthritic conditions.

Osteoarthritis

Osteoarthritis is at least five times more common than rheumatoid arthritis, with over 5 million patients of all ages in the United Kingdom.

The incidence of osteoarthritis increases with age, over the age of 65, 75 per cent of the people have X-ray evidence of the disease, but only 50 per cent have symptoms. Osteoarthritis has been considered to be a part and parcel of the ageing process, i.e. it is considered to be normal wear and tear of ageing. However, this explanation is not acceptable in 1999. Although we do not know the actual cause of this disorder, it seems to be due to several factors, e.g. mechanical overloading, failure of the chondrocyte-controlled internal remodelling system and also factors outside the cartilage, e.g. synovial or vascular changes. Osteoarthritis may start at an early age – in the early 40s or at times even before that. It may complicate, as secondary osteoarthritis, several conditions like Paget's Disease of the bone, rheumatoid arthritis, acromegaly, gout, long-standing corticosteroid therapy and neuropathic arthropathies in diabetes mellitus, syringomyelia and tabes-dorsalis. A strong genetic component is thought to be present, more so in women in whom it is also more common after the age of 55. Powerful drugs and joint replacements have transformed the lives of many arthritic sufferers. Besides, rehabilitation and education are part and parcel of the overall management of arthritic patients. Let me now discuss the management in detail.

Osteoarthritis causes joint pain, stiffness, swelling and limitation of movement of the joint. The disability depends on the number of joints involved and the severity of arthritis. Osteoarthritis can, of course, be generalised.

Managing risk factors
Obesity is an important risk factor – more so in women. Continuing obesity is associated with progression of osteoarthritis, so weight reduction is clearly helpful.

Other risk factors include occupation (farmers and knee bending occupations in men), trauma to the joint including weight bearing sports, as studied in women.

Drug treatment
Simple analgesics like paracetamol may be sufficient; however, if pain is not controlled, compound analgesics like Co-proxamol should be tried. (As compound analgesics tend to give rise to constipation, concomitant use of a laxative may be necessary in many patients.)

Non-steroidal anti-inflammatory drugs (NSAIDs.)
NSAIDS are widely prescribed drugs. Although these drugs are very effective they can cause serious side effects especially in those who are very old. The side effects are mainly related to the upper gastrointestinal system (e.g. from mild indigestion to peptic ulcer, even haemorrhage and perforation), Cardiovascular system (e.g. congestive cardiac failure) and also giddiness and headaches. (please see Appendix). So what could be done to reduce their side effects? There are several options:
1.) To start with, we should prescribe an NSAID only after careful assessment of the severity of the arthritis and other related factors. As mentioned above, simple analgesics (e.g. paracetamol) may be sufficient to control pain.
2.) There are several groups of NSAIDs – some of them have more serious side effects than others. For example, Ibuprofen has fewer side effects com-

pared to other NSAIDs. Diclofenac is another with relatively low risk. (Patients should be informed of possible side effects of NSAIDs).
3.) Doses of NSAID drug can be reduced by combining it with paracetamol.
4.) NSAIDs may be prescribed with other drugs (Proton-Pump Inhibitors, H2 Blocker or Prostaglandin analogue) to reduce side effects.
5.) It is important that patients on an NSAID are reviewed regularly. This measure may not eliminate all the risks of NSAID therapy but will reduce the side effects. Ideally a prescribing physician should know in 'detail' about, say four NSAIDs (more than two dozen NSAIDs are currently available) i.e. one from each group.

Intra-articular injection
This is an effective method for delivering an anti-inflammatory drug, i.e. corticosteroids. Long-acting depot methyl Prednisolone or Triamcinalone are usually used. The intra-articular route (with meticulous sterile technique) is usually helpful for those patients in whom fewer joints are involved. At any rate, injection could be given in the most severely affected joints with benefit. This route is more useful in Rheumatoid Arthritic patients rather than in Osteoarthritics. It does, however, provide symptomatic relief even in the latter. The joints could be injected either in the surgery or in the outpatient clinics, in Day Hospital clinics or even at the patient's home. Repeated injections in the same joint should be avoided.

Apart from corticosteroids, intra-articular hyaluronic acid is also used. Experience of its use in this country is *limited*.

Surgery
Several worthwhile surgical procedures are available, performed for relief of pain, correction of deformity and improvement of functional impairment. Prosthetic hip joint replacement, and now to a large extent knee joint replacement, has revo-

lutionised the management of crippling osteoarthritis of the hip and knee joints. These operations can be useful to a 50-year-old person or to a 95-year-old. Indeed the Queen Mother had a hip replacement operation aged 95 with success. In this context it is worth mentioning Professor Sir John Charnley, one of the most famous sons of Manchester and an Orthopaedic Surgeon of repute. Charnley made an outstanding contribution to the development of total hip replacement. The Centre for Research in Hip Surgery at Wrightington Hospital is a memorial to his life's work.

So what are the indications for hip/knee replacement?
It is the failure of medical treatment with constant pain (including night-time pain) with only one joint mainly involved. Besides, the patient should be reasonably fit and not overweight. Unfortunately the operation is not without complications. These include another operation in about 25 per cent of cases.

Other measures
These include physiotherapy (effort should be directed mainly at improving the range of joint movement) and aids to improve mobility. It is worth remembering that a stick can reduce up to 50 per cent of weight on a joint and is worth trying after careful functional assessment. Apart from these, ultrasound treatment, local cold and hot treatment, hydrotherapy and spa treatment and even acupuncture have been tried with some benefit. Patients may need rehousing to avoid steps and stairs. Patient's education is important too.

Back pain

No description of arthritis will be complete without a mention of backache, a common cause of disability. Many episodes of back pain are mild and self-limiting while others are protracted or recur from time to time and their sufferers have multiple investigations and attend different clinics (e.g.

Rheumatological Outpatients, Orthopaedic Clinics, Pain Clinics, or even alternative medicine clinics) for pain relief.

So what are the main causes of back pain?
Muscles, ligaments, joints, bones and even spinal canal (e.g. in spinal stenosis, narrowing of spinal canal, causing a pinched nerve) may be involved.

For management purposes it is important that back pain is considered under (a) simple back pain (b) nerve root pain and (c) serious pathology. The important causes for back pain are lumbar spondylosis (disc and joint degeneration and lumbar spine area), spinal stenosis (narrowing of spinal canal where nerves are squashed), herniation of intervertebral disc and of course, mechanical strains and sprains; collapsed vertebrae due to osteoporosis, ankylosing spondylitis (usually in younger people), neoplasms (cancers) and at times infection (e.g. acute pyogenic infection or chronic infection due to tuberculosis or very occasionally brucellosis). In many patients magnetic resonance imaging (MRI) is now proving to be very accurate in the diagnosis of back pain. However, this investigation is costly and is not available in every District General Hospital. It is to be preferred also because of no radiation dose, unlike computerised tomography (i.e. CT Scan). At any rate MRI Scan should be urgently arranged if back pain is associated with gait disturbance, urinary incontinence or if the patient has a past history of cancer.

So why may back pain be persistent?
We know that an important risk factor for back pain is a previous history of back pain. Once again, the maxim, prevention is better than cure, is very useful to follow in this context. Lifting technique is very important (as a rough guide, if a load is held at arm's length it will strain the back five times compared to the same load held near the trunk) and so also is the maintenance of sensible posture

during our everyday activities like lying, sitting bending etc. Exercise has an important part to play in the prevention and treatment of acute or chronic back sufferers. In many patients with long standing backache, careful assessment of the patient may reveal depression and psychological factors. Lastly, failed surgery (i.e. surgery to relieve back pain) may well be the reason for intractable back pain. Thus it goes without saying that surgical intervention for herniated discs (most common in adults between 30 and 50 years) and spinal stenosis (those over 65 years mainly) should be undertaken only after due consideration of patient's wishes especially when indications for surgery are not clear-cut.

Rheumatoid arthritis

Active rheumatoid arthritis in the elderly is not common. If present, it is due to flaring up of previously diagnosed rheumatoid arthritis *or* it may arise for the first time in elderly patients. One mainly sees the burnt out cases (of previously diagnosed rheumatoid arthritis) with deformity. There may be superimposed or secondary osteoarthritic changes. Treating rheumatoid arthritis in elderly patients may be problematic because of ever-increasing dangers of bed rest in the elderly, side effects of NSAIDs and need for protracted rehabilitation as they may have concomitant illnesses with polypharmacy (i.e. taking several drugs). Several groups of drugs are available to treat rheumatoid arthritis in middle-aged and elderly patients. Apart from simple analgesics (e.g. paracetamol) and NSAIDS, several disease-modifying drugs may be used either singly or in combinations. A recent issue of the Journal *Age & Ageing* (July 1998) describes the tolerability and toxicity of second-line drug combinations in rheumatoid arthritis in middle-aged and elderly patients: (reviewed in Rheumatology 1997; 1749–54).

All drug combinations (i.e. gold/methotrexate, sulphasalazine/methotrexate. hydroxychloroquine/methotrexate and minocycline/methotrexate) were well tolerated, with usually mild side-effects. Side effects were least common with gold/methotrexate combinations. This should be considered as a guideline only, as this may not relate to an individual patient in clinical practice.

Acute arthritic conditions

Several arthritic and related conditions may present acutely or even as an emergency. They need appropriate management. The conditions include: (Please see table below)

Condition	Management
1. Septic arthritis.	• Joint aspiration • Blood culture • Antibiotics
2. Rheumatoid vasculitis with deep ulcers and gangrene of digits.	• Corticosteroid and cytotoxic drugs
3. Joint effusion following acute synovial rupture, simulating deep venous thrombosis	• Leg elevation and rest • Diagnosis by arthrography, nowadays ideally by MRI
4. Temporal arteritis presenting with headache, visual problems, or even blindness	• High dose Prednisolone, e.g. starting with 60 mg daily
5. Upper gastrointestinal haemorrhage due to peptic ulcer following NSAID therapy	• Blood transfusion • H2 receptor antagonist (Cimetidine or Ranitidine)

Condition	Management
6. Gout – very painful, great toe usually affected, usual precipitating factors are surgery, fasting, diuretics and excessive alcohol intake.	• NSAIDs indicated

There are other acute rheumatological conditions which may present from time to time.

Final message

1. In treating osteoarthritis we should not concentrate on only a joint or joints affected but treat the patient as a whole with drugs, exercises, education, reassurance and ultimately surgery; if indicated.

2. Side effects of drugs used should not be worse than symptoms of primary disease – careful use and supervision of treatment by steroids and NSAIDs should reduce their side effects.

3. It appears that in coming years (a) Magnetic Resonance Imaging will surpass other diagnostic (i.e. imaging) methods for the diagnosis of bad back; however its findings have to be interpreted with great caution, and (b) we may know fundamental aspects of low back pain in more detail.

4. Most people will have back pain and perhaps this should be accepted as part and parcel of normal life. As long as serious conditions like cancer and infection have been ruled out, the condition improves in weeks with conservative measures (i.e. keeping generally active, taking simple pain killers and have perseverence). Most backaches recover, rapidly and substantially.

Useful Addresses:

1. **National Back Pain Association**
The Old Office Block,
Elmtree Road,
Teddington,
Middlesex TW11 8TD
Tel: 0181 977 5474
Fax: 0181 943 5318

2. **Arthritis Care,**
18 Stevenson Way,
London NW1 2HD
Tel: 0171 916 1500

The Association helps arthritis and rheumatism sufferers with useful information and advice regarding aids and other facilities

3. **The Arthritis and Rheumatism Council (A.R.C.),**
St Mary's Court,
St Mary's Gate,
Chesterfield,
Derbyshire S41 7TD
Tel: 01246 558033

Appendix

Side effects of non-steroid anti-inflammatory drugs (NSAIDS) – (12)

Upper gastro-intestinal side effects

1. NSAIDS cause gastric ulcer and erosions of lining of stomach; and bleeding and perforation of both gastric and duodenal ulcers (NSAIDS are responsible for 20–30 per cent of all peptic ulcer complications).

2. Old age, history of upper gastro-intestinal bleeding (or peptic ulceration), short duration or high doses of NSAIDS, and concurrent use of steroids and anticoagulants are known risk factors for upper gastro-intestinal damage due to NSAIDS.

3. Ibuprofen and Fenoprofen are low-risk and Piroxicam, Ketoprofen and Azapropazone are high-risk NSAIDS so far as their upper gastro intestinal toxicity is concerned.

4. Although a history of peptic ulceration is useful before NSAIDs are prescribed, it is worth remembering that (a) there is only a weak relationship between symptom (i.e. what the patient complains of) of peptic ulcer and (b) bleeding can be a first manifestation of a asymptomatic ulcer.

5. Other side-effects

NSAIDS can precipitate cardiac failure and even renal failure and can damage intestinal mucosa. Side effects like rashes, dizziness, vertigo have also been reported.

References/further reading list

1. *Rheumatology*, Part 1 of 2 ; Volume 26:5, 1998 and Part 2 of 2 ; Vol. 26:6, 1998 in *Medicine* (The Medicine Publishing Company Limited).

2. Recent advances: rheumatology by Peter Brooks, *British Medical Journal*, Vol. 316, June 13, 1998 issue (Pages 1810–1812).

3. Initial assessment of back pain : an overview by Alison H. McGregor and Sean P.F. Hughes in *Hospital Medicine*, June 1998 issue.

4. Back pain by Malcom I.V. Jayson in *British Medical Journal*, vol. 313, 10 August 1996.

5. Arthritis and musculo-skeletal disorders by A. Bhalla and B. Shenstone in *A Guide to Care of the Elderly* (Eds. R.B. Shukla and D. Brooks) H.M.S.O. (1996)

6. Care of the elderly in early osteoarthritis - *Geriatric Medicine*, Vol. 27: October 1997.

7. *A Guide to Symptom Relief in Advance Disease* by Claud F.B. Regnard and Sue Tempest, 4th Edition (1998). Published by Hochland and Hochland Ltd.

8. Why does acute back pain become chronic? Editorial. *British Medical Journal*. Vol. 314: June 7, 1997.

9. Locomotor problems, in *Lecture Notes on Geriatrics* by N. Coni and S. Webster, Fifth Edition, 1998; Blackwell Science.

10. Route of drug administration: intra articular route by Thomas Pullar in *Prescriber's Journal* 1998, Vol. 38 (Pages 123–126); The Stationary Office.

11. Rheumatological emergencies. Maddison, P. *Medicine International* Vol 2, October 1985 issue, Pages 901–905).

12. *Medicine – Gastroenterology* issue Part 1, July, 1998. The Medicine Publishing Co. Limited.

13. Low-back pain by Richard A. Deyo in *Scientific American*, August, 1998 issue; Pages 28–33.

Infections in the Elderly

CHAPTER 8

Elderly patients are affected by infections in a significant way. Pneumonia (which is a most common cause of urgent hospital admissions), urinary tract infections, and skin and soft tissue infections (e.g. cellulitis, boils, carbuncles) are some of the more common infections seen in elderly people. Often, these infections lead to bacteraemia (i.e. presence of bacteria in the blood but often transient, and condition not necessarily serious) or septicaemia (i.e micro-organisms in the blood with high temperature and shivering and a serious condition) resulting in greater mortality in this age-group.

With advancing years, the body defences (which are the immune response to infection) become weaker and the quality and quantity of antibodies (substances in the blood which neutralize or destroy bacteria) decrease and so also does the lymphocyte function. These changes could affect the way the disease presents. Thus the symptoms such as temperature and rise in polymorphonuclear leucocytes may not be marked, thus making the diagnosis of infection difficult.

Doctors looking after elderly patients are used to suspect infection in their patients by finding non-specific symptoms like urinary incontinence, being unwell with lack of interest and socialisation and even falls. Often drugs, such as steroids, antacids and even antibiotics may in fact help infection to occur. Besides, age-related changes in various body-systems may lead to increased incidence of infections in elderly patients. One classical example is aspiration pneumonia which may be secondary to factors like poor swallowing, inefficient breathing and poor mobility. Likewise, increased incidence of urinary tract infections in the elderly may be due to factors like age-related changes in the bladder, poor fluid intake and prostate enlargement in men. Disorders such as diabetes, presence of prosthesis and other invasive devices such as catheters further help bacteria to breach the already weakened defences. Often a large number of elderly patients are prescribed antibiotics as a firm diagnosis cannot be made. If the suspicion of infection is high, the appropriate samples (e.g. midstream urine, sputum and even blood) should be taken prior to administration of any antibiotic.

Happily, treatment of infections differs in one fundamental way from treatment of other diseases in that infections can be more effectively treated by antibiotics, i.e. cured.

In this short article, only common infections – pneumonia and UTI (urinary tract infection) will mainly be discussed. Mention will also be made of other less common infections (cellulitis and shingles), some special infections (MRSA, one of the super bugs and *Clostridium difficile* infection) and the all important topical issue of 'antibiotic resistance'.

Modes of transmission of various infections

There are many which include:

1. Air-borne infection (e.g. coughing and sneezing) – influenza, tuberculosis.
2. By food and water – hepatitis A, dysentry and typhoid (when travelling abroad in many countries).
3. Sexually transmitted – HIV infection
4. Insect transmission – malaria (problem for travellers)
5. Animal transmission – Rabies (not relevant in U.K.)
6. Blood-borne – HIV infection, hepatitis B & C

It follows from the above that following travel, infections like typhoid, malaria, giardiasis, amoebiasis and traveller's diarrhoea may be imported to this country.

Investigations in common infections

Blood culture is one of the most valuable investigations, at least two sets should be taken in any suspected infection as a positive result would be very significant. A mid-stream specimen of urine (MSSU) for microscopy and culture, a sample of sputum for microscopy and culture are less valuable as the significance of some results would not be conclusive because of the presence of normal flora/the contamination of the sample in the process of collecting it. Sputum samples should be collected with the assistance of a physiotherapist. 'In and Out' catheterisation is justifiable in getting a sample of urine specially from 'not so co-operative' patients as the resistance pattern of uropathogen could be very variable as a result of previous catheterisation and antibiotic therapy.

Empirical antibiotics

Antibiotic use in the elderly is very common as infections are difficult to diagnose. Meningitis or septic-arthritis could often be diagnosed with confidence even without laboratory investigations. Chest infection and UTI may not be obvious but every effort should be made to locate the system that may be involved and tailor the antibiotics to the organism that might be responsible for an infection in the particular system, rather than using a broad spectrum antibiotic for all situations which could then lean to antibiotic-associated diarrhoea.

Chest infection/pneumonia

The normal flora of the upper respiratory tract such as *Streptococcus pneumoniae*, *Haemophilus influenzae* and *Moraxella catarrhalis* are potential pathogens to the lower respiratory tract. In the elderly, Gram-negative bacilli and *Staphylococcus aureus* colonise this region and should be given due recognition, especially in residents in nursing homes. Only about 5% of all lower respiratory infections are pneumonias. *S. pneumoniae* is one of the commonest causes of pneumonia, especially lobar pneumonia acquired in the community. Often tachypnoea may be the only likely sign, a chest X-ray could confirm the diagnosis. As a bacteriological diagnosis is valuable, blood cultures and samples of sputum for culture are indicated. In a seriously ill patient urgent sputum microscopy Gram film may show organisms resembling pneumococci supporting the X-ray findings and help in the selection of antibiotics.

A mild pneumonia in a stable patient could be managed in the community and the drug of choice would be Penicillin.

Seriously ill patients may need to be admitted to hospital and managed according to the British Thoracic Society Guidelines especially when no specific diagnosis is available and the antibiotics should be selected to cover all possible pathogens. Cefuroxime and Erythromycin are the recommended antibiotics.

Community-acquired Pneumonia

Organisms found are:

- *Streptococci pneumoniae* – most common (about 35 per cent)
- Atypical organisms (*Mycoplasma pneumonia, Chlamydia pneumonia* and *Legionella* (*Mycoplasma pneumonia* – in epidemic years, occurring every 4 years or so)
- *Haemophilus influenzae* (8–10 per cent)
- *Moraxella cararrhalis*
- *Staphylococcus aureus* – post influenzae
- *Klebsiella* and other coliforms
- Anaerobes – Aspiration pneumonia
- Influenzae virus
- *Pneumocystic carinii* – in AIDS (HIV infections)

Antibiotics in Community-acquired Pneumonia

- Benzylpenicillin
- Ampicillin
- Erythromycin/Clarithromycin
- Cephalosporin – Cefuroxime or Cefotaxime
- Co-amoxiclav
- Levofloxacin, a quinolone available for both intravenous and oral use (effective in Gram positive and atypical organisms).

Hospital-acquired Pneumonia

Hospitals are hostile environments for the elderly, – pressure to use many antibiotics may promote the emergence of multi-resistant bacteria. Gram-negative bacteria such as, *E. coli, K. pneumonia* and *Pseudomonas aeruginosa*, are liable to colonise the upper respiratory tract and secondarily invade the lower respiratory tract.

Nebulisers and other devices and invasive procedures and the use of antibiotics further help in colonising URT (upper respiratory tract)with Gram negative bacteria of hospital origin.

Microscopy and cultures of freshly taken samples of sputum and blood for cultures are the more useful investigations. As the results of these cultures will not be available for 24–48 hours, they should be started on a Cephalosporin or a broad spectrum Penicillin plus an aminoglycoside should be adequate in most instances.

Urinary tract infection (UTI)

This is a common problem in the elderly. Incomplete bladder emptying is one of the key factors in the pathogenesis of UTI in this age group. Obstruction and catheterisation, immobility, decreased mental and physical state are the major contributory factors in the development of bacteriuria.

Long-term catheterisation of the bladder inevitably leads to colonisation of the bladder with bacteria, which subsequently leads to a bacteraemia or the infection could ascend up the ureters to infect the kidney. Therefore the decision to catheterise a patient should not be taken too lightly.

In the female the perineum is inevitably colonised by coliform bacteria from the gut and the short urethra is not a sufficient barrier to prevent the migration of the bacteria to the bladder.

In men even the condom catheter drainage is known to predispose to UTI.

The microbiology of UTIs

E. Coli is usually the commonest organism followed by *proteus* sp. and *Klebsiella* sp. but in patients who had been catheterised or have been on antibiotics the more resistant Gram-negative bacteria such as *Enterobacter* and *Pseudomonas* may be seen in a proportion of such patients.

Antibiotics prescribed in UTI

These are Trimethoprim, Nitrofurantoin, Cephalexin, Ampicillin and Fluoroquinolones.

Fifteen to 20 per cent of women aged 65–70 have significant bacteria in their urine without symptoms of urinary infection (asymptomatic bacteriuria). It is probably unnecessary to treat women over 65 with asymptomatic bacteriuria.

In general, infections may take longer to clear in elderly patients (over 65 years) than in younger women. Ampicillin/Amoxycillin should not be used in the blind therapy of urinary tract infection as in most hospitals 30% or more of the coliforms would be resistant to these antibiotics. Antibiotics used as blind therapy should be based on the local sensitivity pattern. Usually Trimethoprim would suffice. (In infections due to bacteria which are resistent to Trimethoprim, up to 90 per cent of pathogens (bacteria) may be sensitive, i.e. respond to, Co-amoxiclave).

Less common infections

Cellulitis

The infection involves a localised area of the skin (it is subcutaneous, i.e. under the skin). Several organisms are responsible for causing cellulitis but *S. pyogenes* is most important. The area affected is painful, red and is raised and there may not be a clear cut margin. The cause of the entry of organism may not be known.

Treatment is by Penicillin given by mouth (intravenously if infection is severe). Erythromycin should be given to those who are allergic to Penicillin. Local application of antibiotics should be avoided as it does not help.

Shingles (Herpes Zoster)

This condition is progressively more common in older people and is due to reactivation of a latent varicella zoster virus (VZV). Drugs, diseases, advancing age and depressed immunity (cell-mediated immunity) promote reactivation. The condition starts with pain for a few days in an area of skin followed by red patches with vesicles, then pustules followed by scab formation. Usually a single dermatome is affected and the condition may last altogether for up to 4 weeks.

There are several drugs to treat this painful condition. These are:

1. Aciclovir 800 mg five times a day for 7 days
2. Famciclovir, 250 mgs three times a day for 7 days
3. Valaciclovir 1 g three times a day for 7 days

Prompt early treatment (i.e. given within 24 hours of appearance of rash) can reduce both the severity of future longstanding pain, i.e. post-herpetic neuralgia (see chapter on Aches and Pain, Pins and Needles) and shorten the duration of illness. Adequate pain control is essential

Special infections

MRSA (Methicillin-resistant *Staphylococcus aureus*, is one of the 'superbugs')

This is the name given to *Staphylococcus aureus* isolates that are resistant to Methicillin Flucloxacillin, Cloxacillin and also the Cephalosporins, often they can be resistant to Erythromycin, Tetracycline and Ciprofloxacin.

Over the last 5–7 years a large number of hospitals have been affected by this organism. The elderly are at a higher risk of being colonised by this organism because of their high dependency, bed sores, venous ulcers and urinary catheters. Attendant's hands are thought to be the commonest route of transmission. When the patients are in acute medical wards, screening should be carried out by the Infection Control Nurse and attempts should be made to eradicate the organism from those found to be colonised. The local guidelines should be followed as the protocols may differ from hospital to hospital and from one type of ward to another. The most important factor in the prevention of spread is thought to be good hand washing with soap and water. Fortunately severe infections such as septicaemia and chest infection, with MRSA are rare but if found, these would need to be treated with Vancomycin or Teicoplanin. Where a person is colonised and the infection needs to be eradicated, Mupirocin and Triclosan or similar products could be used. Effort should be made to remove causes of cross-infection (overcrowding, poor staffing and poor hygeine). Only patients with uncontainable secretions should be isolated. In general, spread within nursing homes is relatively infrequent and infection is rare.

Clostridium difficile (Antibiotic-associated diarrhoea)
Pseudomembranous colitis is the result of the action of the toxin produced by an over growth of *Clostridium difficile* in the colon. Often the use or over use of antibiotics, especially the Cephalosporins and the Penicillins such as Ampicillin and Amoxycillin, lead to this condition. Infection control techniques such as improved hygiene, especially good hand washing practices, help to stop an outbreak. In the management of such patients it is important to stop all antibiotics that are not essential and that are of doubtful value. The infection due to *C. difficile* is a continuing problem in hospital. Unfortunately it is now seen in the community as well.

Management of C. difficile infection
Thus the basis of controlling infection is careful antibiotic prescribing and simple hygeine measures. Management includes the following:
1. High standard of personal hygiene in patients, staff and family carers should be encouraged. These practices help to stop an outbreak.
2. Antibiotics, which are not essential or are of doubtful value, should be stopped. At any rate, prescribing third generation cephalosporins in vulnerable patients (frail, especially nursing home patients) should be avoided.
3. Patients who have symptoms should be isolated.

4. Oral Metronidazole (Flagyl) in the doses of 400 mg three times a day for 7 to 10 days is the treatment of choice. Oral Vancomycin (dose 125 mg three times a day) is a considerably more expensive alternative.

Tuberculosis
A brief mention of infection by *Mycobacterium tuberculosis* is in order. This should always be suspected in patients with a history of loss of weight, malaise and unexplained fever with poor nutrition, general frailty and presence of other diseases, e.g. diabetes. (It is not true that it affects only people of ethnic origin. Patients with decalcification of healed and calcified tuberculous lesions (that is where sputum contains AAFB – alcohol and acid fast bacillus) should be isolated and managed in a single room with exhaust ventilation if available, for two weeks and should be under the care of a Chest Physician or Chest Clinic, where they could be followed up. A therapeutic trial with anti-tuberculous drug may be justified in a patient where TB is strongly suspected and other investigations have been negative and result of sputum-culture is awaited. It is a notifiable disease.

Preventing infections
Recurrent cystitis may be preventable if low-dose Trimethoprim or Nitrofurantoin are taken for 3 to 6 months.

Role of vaccinations
Two vaccinations need special mention here:
1. Influenza vaccination, which should be given once a year to adults, e.g. those who are 75 and above. However, younger high-risk patients should be vaccinated too.
2. Pneumococcal vaccine should be given every 5 years or so to people with diabetes, cardiac disease, chronic bronchitis, kidney failure and to those who have had their spleen removed for medical reasons.

Besides the above, hepatitis A, diphtheria and polio vaccine should be given to those travelling abroad to endemic areas with these diseases.

Antibiotic resistance

Bacteria are becoming increasingly resistant to antibiotics. This is potentially a major public health problem. There is no doubt that over prescription of antibiotics is the cause of infection by superbugs. Efforts by all concerned should be made to halt the progress of this threat. Careful consideration should be given while prescribing antibiotics to patients especially with chest infections as many of these infections are due to viruses where antibiotics should not be prescribed. In fact, up to 50 per cent of antibiotic prescriptions (mostly prescribed by General Practitioners) may be unnecessary. Over the counter sale of antibiotics may have complicated the issue further. All in all, apart from education to doctors and patients, public health measures, regulatory controls, surveillance (a surveillance system for Europe is already in place but a global co-operation on surveillance will be necessary) and further research is needed to stem the tide of this global threat. A tighter guideline on antibiotic uses is needed and may well come about soon.

Summary

1. There have been considerable changes in the prevention of community- and hospital-acquired infections during the last 25 years.
2. Many chest infections seen by General Practitioners are self-limiting and do not need antibiotics. Only a small percentage (about 5 per cent) of patients with lower respiratory tract infections have pneumonia. (The problem is there is no clear cut criteria to absolutely differentiate between a patient with pneumonia and the one with lower respiratory infection.)
3. Diagnosing urinary tract infections in elderly patients is an important problem. Continued reliance on culture and sensitivity of a sample of midstream urine is essential.
4. Every effort should be made to reduce the increasing incidence of resistant organisms which is gradually assuming a public health problem. Prudent prescribing, education, surveillance, infection control and last but not least, development of newer antimicrobials including those which can conquer 'superbugs' are main current and future strategies.
5. With the explosion in international travel, there is now increased chance of contracting infections and importing infections into the U.K. (Travel medicine is now attracting increasing attention.)

Final message

1. Extra care is needed to diagnose pneumonia and urinary tract infection in the elderly.
2. Rational use of antibiotics (i.e. eliciting need for starting treatment and history of allergy, establishing proper route and duration of treatment and seeking advice of microbiologists, where necessary) is essential to provide maximum benefit to patients, reduce antibiotic resistance and not to mention, contain cost.

References/Further reading list

1. Cummings D. M. *et al.* (1990) Antibiotics for common infections in the elderly. *Prim. Care*, 17 : 883–903

2. Infectious Disease I in *Journal of The Royal College of Physician of London* Vol.32 (May/June 1998).

3. Norman D. C. (1991) Pneumonia in the Elderly. *Geriatric* 46 : 26–32

4. *C. difficile* by Mark H. Wilcox in *Geriatric Medicine* September 1998 issue (Page 31–34)

5. Henschke P. J. (1993) Infections in the Elderly. *Med. J. Australia* 158: 830–834

6. Commentary. *Age and Ageing* 1997 ; 26: 165– 168

7. Woodhead M. (1994) Pneumonia in the Elderly. *J.A.C.* 34 ; Suppl : 85–92.

8. *Lecture Notes in Infectious Disease* (B.K. Mandal *et al.*) Fifth Edition, Blackwell Science, 1996.

9. Management of Urinary Tract Infection in Women. *Drug and Therapeutic Bulletin*. Vol. 36, No. 4, April 1998.

10. Antimicrobial resistance. Editorial, *British Medical Journal*, 5 Sept. 1998; Vol 317: 609–610

11. Antibiotic Treatment of Adults with Chest Infection in General Practice. *Drug and Therapeutic Bulletin* Vol. 36, Sept. 1998 issue.

12. Superbugs: are we at the threshold of a new dark age? Editorial, *Hospital Medicine* July, 1998, Vol. 59 524–526

13. *Churchill's Pocketbook of Clinical Microbiology* (T.J.J. Inglis) £15.00 P.B. 185 Pages.

Acknowledgement

I am grateful to Dr B.S. Perera, Consultant Microbiologist, Royal Oldham Hospital, Oldham for his valuable contribution in preparing this article.

Elderly Driver

Age, inlcuding physical frailty as such, is no bar to holding a licence. Contrary to stereotype, the elderly are not bad drivers – they have learnt to regulate themselves, i.e. how far to drive, when to drive and where to drive. The AA predicts a boom in elderly licence holders in the new millennium. D.V.L.A. (Driver and Vehicle Licencing Agency) require at the age of 70 that no medical disability is present. Thereafter, every three years a licence is issued, subject to satisfactory completion of medical questions on the application form. As ageing progresses, a driver or his relatives may be aware that the combination of progressive loss of memory, impairment in concentration and reaction time with possible loss of confidence, suggest consideration be given to stop driving.

After years of experience, many pensioners retain their good driving skills. AA wants to see a panel of doctors, insurance companies and motoring organisations set up to give advice and information to the elderly about their driving abilities.

References: 1. For Medical Practitioners. *At a glance Guide to Current Medical Standard of Fitness to Drive*; issued by Drivers Medical Unit D.V.L.A., Swansea; March 1998.
2. *The Times*, Sept. 19, 1998.

Management of Headaches

CHAPTER 9

Headache is very common. In fact, few of us will have escaped it. Happily, most headaches are benign (they could be disabling nevertheless) i.e. they are not of sinister significance and are not due to structural lesions of the brain. The causes of headache are diverse: these range from trivial, such as due to eating ice cream or a Chinese meal, drinking a glass of wine, following a severe bout of coughing, (say, following a viral infection) to dental or facial pain, migraine and tension headaches (by far the commonest cause of headache) and not forgetting approximately 1 per cent of cases due to sinister causes like haemorrhage in the brain (subarachnoid or in the brain itself), meningitis or brain tumour or head injury. Very occasionally a patient with an intractable undiagnosed headache may consult several Specialists, e.g. General Physician, Neurologist, Dental Surgeon, Ophthalmologist, E.N.T., (Ear, nose and throat) Specialist, Psychiatrist and even a Specialist in alternative medicine.

So why do we get headache?

We experience headache when the nerve supply to the head is involved in processes like stretching, inflammation or even distortion. The nerves involved are mainly:-

1. trigeminal
2. glossopharyngeal
3. vagus
4. upper cervical (pertaining to upper part of the back of the neck)

Thus, although the headache could be due to involvement of the brain or structures outside it, most headaches are, in fact, due to causes outside the brain. This is why most headaches have an excellent outcome. Finally, although most of the brain is not sensitive to painful stimuli, the site of a possible source of headache is the mid-brain.

I will now briefly describe some important (but by no means, all common) causes of headache:

Migraine headache

Migraine headache has been known for about 5,000 years. It is very common. It is more common in women. The headache is severe, episodic and usually felt on one side of the face. It may last from a few hours to three days. There are usually triggering factors for headache: stress, loud noise, hunger, bright light (television) items of food, hormones (pills, menstruation, pregnancy and menopause) and many others. Even movement of the head aggravates the pain. This may be the reason why sufferers like complete rest in a darkened room. Treatment exists both for acute attacks (painkillers or Sumatriptan (Imigran) and for prophylaxis (if attacks are frequent) with drugs like Pizotifen, Valproate and Propranolol (Propranolol not to be given to asthmatics of course).

Tension headache
Here, pain which comes on and builds slowly, is a tight and bandlike discomfort. The muscles in the back of the neck feel tight. The pain may go on for many days. The severity of the headache varies. It is not correct to say that most such patients have anxiety/depression – only some patients have them.

Cluster headache
This is also called migrainous neuralgia. Men, (usually 30–50 years old) are affected 10 times more than women. The pain – described variously as stabbing or lancing – starts at night and is felt behind one eye. The affected eye may look red and that side of the nostril feels blocked. The duration of pain is not more than half an hour or so. They return at the same time the following night and can last several weeks. The cluster returns up to two to three times a year approximately. Experts now consider this type of headache to be triggered by nerves rather than being vascular in nature.

Temporal arteritis
This is the inflammatory disorder of the artery involved and is common in later life, i.e. beyond 50 years. It is more common in women than men. The pain is felt in the artery while brushing hair or resting the head on a pillow. It is essential that this condition is promptly recognised and treated (with steroids), otherwise half of the untreated patients will develop blindness. While many patients have temporal artery biopsy to arrive at the diagnosis, in others raised ESR (erythrocyte sedimentation rate) and prompt relief with high doses of steroids is all that is needed, in view of the seriousness of the condition.

Headache due to involvement of extracranial structures: i.e. teeth, eye, sinuses and upper cervical spine (part of the back of the neck)
The conditions include dental pain (probably the most common cause of facial pain), glaucoma, sinusitis and arthritis of the back of the neck.

Headache due to meningitis/subarachnoid haemorrhage
In subarachnoid haemorrhage, the headache is sudden and severe. CT scan of the brain is the investigation of choice. In case of meningitis there is fever, malaise and additionally skin rashes may be seen. Lumbar puncture is usually indicated to diagnose meningitis and prompt treatment with antibiotics instituted, if meningitis is bacterial.

Brain tumour headache
Here the patients experience dull headache which is intermittent to start with. Typically, the headache is said to occur during early mornings. In course of time it becomes persistent and may be associated with sickness. Activities like coughing and bending make the headache worse. CT scan of the brain should be arranged.

Headache following lumbar puncture (LP)
Lumbar puncture is commonly performed to diagnose a neurological disorder or in spinal anaesthesia. Over 30% of the patients complain of headache when a 20G bevelled needle is used. The headache is usually experienced 24–48 hours after the LP and can be severe and is due to leakage of the cerebrospinal fluid.

A British Medical Journal Editorial (22 Nov. 1997) suggested that if a 22G blunt needle is used for LP, the post LP headache will be reduced by sixfold i.e. down to 5 per cent. Although the new needles are expensive, the cost will be more than offset by treating fewer patients with headaches due to. Clearly this very effective way of preventing LP headache should not be ignored.

General comments regarding management of headaches

1. As is obvious from the above account, very few patients need special investigations like CT brain scan or magnetic resonance imaging of the brain.
2. Most headaches are self-limiting – we do not stop eating ice cream or a Chinese meal (it is thought to be due to sodium glutamate in the food). In due course one uses the trick to avoid the headache.
3. Patients need to be reassured, especially those with recurrent disabling headaches like migraine and cluster headaches.
4. Contrary to the general belief most patients with hypertension do not usually suffer from headache. When hypertension is severe and where a patient is anxious and worried about it, he/she will have headache then.
5. Most cases of headaches in the hospital setting, can be managed by General Physicians/Geriatricians. However, occasionally an expert opinion (e.g. a Neurologist's) is needed, especially for obscure neurological problems, intractable migraine, head injury etc. A lot, however, depends on local arrangement.
6. Depending upon the type of headache, patients need the necessary treatment e.g. pain killers and specific medication in migraine, antiobiotics in bacterial meningitis and sinusitis and surgery in brain tumour and so on.
7. Many drugs are known to have headache as their side effect. For example, nitrate to treat angina can give rise to headache. In such situations, drug-dose should be reduced or the drug even stopped, and if indicated, an alternative drug prescribed. But

things are not as easy as they seem. I recall an elderly patient who had this 'side effect', who turned out to have not only common arthritis of the back of the neck but was also subsequently diagnosed to have temporal arteritis. When treated with analgesics and steroids and a collar, she was free from headache and her quality of life improved remarkably. Thus, multiple pathologies for the same symptom should not be forgotten in elderly patients.
8. These days one often talks about evidence-based medicine in management of diseases. While there is nothing wrong with it, the doctor should not be carried away because an individual patient may not be covered by the 'evidence'. So, the doctor should manage an individual patient on its own merit or circumstances. This clearly helps the patient. This approach is combined evidence-based and common sense medicine.
9. In a patient (especially an elderly patient) with headache and with comparatively recent onset of dementia, one should consider the possibility of chronic subdural haematoma. The head injury is so trivial in 1/3 to 1/2 of such cases that history of injury is not present. A CT scan of the brain should be arranged.
10. New Developments
Apart from CT brain scan and magnetic resonance imaging of the brain, new methods to deal with patients with brain tumour, head injury and subarachnoid haemorrhage, are being used. These include trans-cranial doppler (TCD) and its modification, colour-coded duplex sonography.

Final message

1. To diagnose the cause of headache correctly, a meticulous history (history of duration of headache being the most important) and examination of the patient is of the utmost importance. Eventually this saves time and money spent on unnecessary investigations.

2. Although the outcome of most headaches is excellent, many patients may be quite disabled with it. Discussion with the patient regarding the nature of headache and reassurance should be part and parcel of overall management.

3. Headaches which (a) are severe and of sudden onset, (b) are accompanied by fever and rashes, (c) have neurological signs with or without altered consciousness, need investigations without delay.

Useful address

British Migraine Association
178a High Road,
Byfleet,
Westbyfleet,
Surrey KT14 7ED

References/Further reading list

1. *Cecil Text Book of Medicine* 19th Edition (1992)

2. *British Medical Journal* November 22, 1997 issue

3. *Harrison's Principals of Internal Medicine* 14th Edition 1998

4. *Lancet*, February 1998 issue

5. *Headache – Problems in Diagnosis and Treatment* edited by Anthony Hopkins, W.B. Saunders Co London, 1988.

6. *Lancet* Vol 351 1998 P275 (quoted in *New Scientist*, 1 August 1998)

Useful booklets

1. *Headache – A Guide to Headache: Causes and Treatments* (A British Brain and Spine Foundation Neurological Disorders Booklet 1998).

2. *Brain Tumour – A guide for Patients and Carers*. (A British Brain and Spine Foundation Neurological Disorders Booklet 1998).

Dementia (Alzheimers's Disease)

CHAPTER 10

An estimated 3 million Europeans have Alzheimer's disease (1). Although its incidence is more or less steady, its prevalence is increasing, both in developed and in developing countries (incidentally, incidence is as they arrive and prevalence is as they are found). It is suggested that as the prevalence of this disease roughly doubles every 5 years, it reaches 32 per cent among people aged 90.

Size of the problem

For the next 25 years or so, the population of elderly over 75 years, and especially those over 85 years, will increase faster than the elderly group of 65 years as a whole.

With the population of the United Kingdom over 56 million – and some 15 per cent of these over 65 years – it is not difficult to realise the immense problems to be faced in managing patients with dementia.

So what is dementia?

Alzheimer's dementia is not a natural part of the ageing process. It is usually an irreversible and progressive destruction of the brain in old age. (Not all cases of dementia, however, occur in old age. If it occurs in people under 65 years of age, it is called presenile dementia).

There is decline of intellect, behaviour and personality and it is slowly progressive. The patients are unaware of this progressive loss of memory and personality but those closest to them are affected most with despair and surprise. The condition differentiates patients with generalised cognitive (memory, language, personality) impairment, from those with other confusional states or focal lesions.

Alzheimer's disease and dementia should not be considered as synonymous – although Alzheimer's disease is the commonest cause of dementia; it is responsible for the dementia in over half of all cases.

Other causes of dementia are vascular dementias (also called multi-infarct dementia, occurring after several strokes and usually associated with hypertension), delayed effects of head injury, neurosyphilis (general paralysis of the insane, now rare), AIDS, alcoholism, hypothyroidism, kidney failure and dialysis dementia, carcinoma of the brain and meninges, pernicious anaemia and other less common conditions. Recently a bacterium has been incriminated as its possible association with Alzheimer's dementia. This needs further study. Every effort should be made to look for a treatable cause of dementia in an otherwise fit person. One such example is normal pressure hydrocephalus which is treated by a shunt operation.

What causes dementia?

Alzheimer's disease and vascular causes remain the major causes of dementia and may coexist. As Alzheimer's disease is the commonest cause of dementia over half a million people in the United Kingdom may be affected.

In Alzheimer's disease there is an accumulation of neurofibrillary tangles and protein plaques of B amyloid in the brain. It is thought that the deposits of these proteins cause disruption of function of brain cells and may themselves be a by-product of dying neurons. Apart from this, other factors which have been incriminated as causes of dementia are toxins (e.g. aluminium is now once again thought to be a cause), an infectious agent, an abnormal protein, and deficit of cholinergic and other transmitter systems in the brain.

Diagnosis of Alzheimer's Disease

A clear cut painstaking history is very helpful, memory impairment being an early feature. Many conditions simulate Alzheimer's disease and these must be ruled out.

They include various confusional states and depression (depressive pseudodementia).

A formal mental testing is necessary, which gives a rough idea of his/her memory, orientation etc. Also, routine laboratory tests may be normal so it is mostly by excluding other conditions that the diagnosis is arrived at.

Specialised investigations include CT scan (computerised tomography scanning) of brain, MRI (magnetic resonance imaging) and PET (positron emission tomography). The last two are usually not available in many District General Hospitals.

CT scanning of the brain is a non-traumatic investigation and does effectively exclude other causes of dementia, i.e. tumours, strokes and normal pressure hydrocephalus. It provides important information about atrophy of the cerebral cortex and size of ventricles of the brain.

An EEG (electroencephalogram) does help to exclude epilepsy but on the whole it does not assist much in diagnosis. A specific test for Alzheimer's disease does not, as yet, exist. However, researches to find a cause for Alzheimer's disease continues.

A definite diagnosis is made by looking at the histology of brain tissue. Unfortunately this is usually done at post-mortem. (The histological changes include neurofibrillary tangles and senile plaques.)

It is very important that the patients and their families are told as fully as possible about the nature of the illness (average lifespan 10 years) and its possible future management. Failure to do so not only leads to their dissatisfaction but may adversely affect the subsequent management of the patient. It is also helpful to provide them with information about family publications, on looking after a patient with dementia. (A valuable book for the relatives and carers of those suffering from dementia is *Caring at Home* by Nancy Kohner. This publication is by the National Extension College, 18 Brooklands Avenue, Cambridge CB2 2HN).

Protective Factors for Alzheimer's Disease

Non-smoking, non-steroidal anti-inflammatory drugs, hormone replacement and education are said to be protective factors (3). Wine is protective too.

Management of Alzheimer's disease

Drug treatment

No specific drug to treat Alzheimer's disease is currently available (an ideal drug will be the one which can prevent deposition of amyloid in the brain). So current drug treatment is aimed at (a) behavioural problems like sleep disturbances, wandering and aggression, or (b) symptomatic treatment of dementia itself.

1. *Behavioural problems/disturbances* are due to several factors and include changes due to environment, other disease present, i.e. medical illnesses giving rise to delirium (examples are transient ischaemic attacks or mini-strokes, infections mainly of chest, but also of urinary tract and constipation and various medications). Management includes treating any medical condition or depression (Haloperidol in small doses, e.g. 0.5 mg or Thioridazine (Melleril) 10 mg may help. Help from a Clinical Psychologist or even Psychiatrist may be needed.

2. *Symptomatic Treatment of Alzheimer's disease*

Two drugs are now available – Donepezil and Rivastigmine. Both are acetylcholinesterase inhibitors and thus work by increasing the amount of acetylcholine, especially in those areas of the brain which are mainly concerned with memory and thinking, (e.g. cortical area and hippocampus). On current indications both these drugs appear to be effective symptomatic treatment for dementia due to Alzheimer's disease. (5)

After full assessment, patients found eligible (mini-mental score should be between 10 and 26) are given the drug for 3 months initially to find out if they are benefiting. Clearly, if there is no clear evidence of benefit, there is no need to continue the drug. As the incidence of dementia increases as one grows older (and there is already an increase in our elderly population), there are clearly significant cost-implications of treating such patients. As the residential-care constitutes the main cost of their care, prescribing these drugs will, in suitable patients, bring down or delay the number of such patients (half of all patients suffering from Alzheimer's dementia may benefit) entering nursing homes. It is suggested that SMAC (Standing Medical Advisory Committee) Guidelines currently available for Donepezil, i.e. Aricept, should be followed (please see Appendix 2 for the main points of this Guideline)

Community care

The concept of community care is, of course, not new and has been talked about for over 35 years. Sir Roy Griffiths has rightly summed up this approach thus: 'If community care means anything, it is that the responsibility is placed as near to the individual and his carers as possible.'

This is the perfect approach for the care of demented people in the community; but it has meaning only if the local authorities are able to set local priorities with finite funding available.

Also an adequate preparation has to be made to support such patients in the community. The improvements in the imaginative housing programmes and various support systems are to be welcomed. Care of the carers should form an important part of the management of such patients. The carers deserve support and this should be provided for them – the latest Government initiative in this respect should be welcomed.

Current research

After a lull of several decades, the research of Alzheimer's disease has really taken off. Happily the current research is quite extensive, directed not only at the diagnosis and cause of this condition but also at general management:

1. Genetics of Alzheimer's disease – At present only one genetic factor, without any doubt, is linked with late onset of Alzheimer's disease and this is e4 allele of apolipoprotein E. But apolipoprotein E e4 is neither sufficient nor necessary to cause

Alzheimer's disease. To complicate the matter further a whole string of genetic associations with late onset Alzheimer's disease have been recorded by various groups. So where do we go from here so far as a specific treatment is concerned? The answer is that until disease slowing treatments are available there appears to be no need for predictive testing based on various genes (apolipoprotein E, d2 macroglobulin or any other genes).

2. identifying the new protein in the neurofibrillary tangle; (c) looking for distinctive early impairment such as olfactory, visual fields, and word-finding; (d) identifying different patterns in the disease and trying to relate them to biochemical and histological findings of the brain; (e) investigating the cerebral metabolism in the disorder by using PET (positron emission tomography); (f) finding novel forms of community and institutional care; and (g) investigating how carers may be helped to cope.

Government supports the care and treatment of Alzheimer's disease through the National Health Service, social security payments and grants to local authorities. It does so indirectly through its contribution to the Medical Research Council, King's Fund, Mental Health Foundation for Age Research, Health Service Research, Age Concern, The Alzheimer's Disease Society, MIND etc.

It should however be stated that the support is proportionately very much less than that provided by the USA which has a small percentage of elderly population. All in all a good liaison between all the involved professionals – doctors, social services, community psychiatric nurses, clinical psychologists, psychotherapists, physiotherapists, speech therapists, occupational therapists, chiropodists, voluntary organisations and last but not least, friends and neighbours – needs to be further strengthened.

Dementias – summary of management

1. As confusional states are not synonymous with dementia, all confused patients should not be labelled as demented.

2. Common causes of dementia are Alzheimer's, vascular, mixed dementias and diffuse Lewy Body Dementia. The most important risk factor for dementia is advanced age – at least 1 in 5 people beyond 80 years show cognitive impairment.

3. In the diagnosis of dementia we need:
   a. careful history and physical examination
   b. Mini-Mental State Examination (see Appendix) and,
   c. ideally, brain imaging by CT or MRI
   and also,
   d. Genetic risk factors are increasingly being recognised.

4. Vascular dementia (about 10 per cent) is usually underdiagnosed because:
   a. there may be absence of neurological signs or even no finding on CT Brain Scan
   b. assigned a diagnosis of stroke and hence not counted.

5. Patients with significant dementia usually attend outpatients with a relative/carer and hardly complain of their symptoms.

6. Dementia of Lewy Body Type may well be the second most important cause of dementia (15–20 per cent) of dementia, on post-mortem) characterised by clouding of consciousness, Parkinsonian symptoms, recent memory loss less severely impaired and different psychotic symptoms including hallucinations.

7. Delirium and depression may be wrongly diagnosed in dementia. In fact, depression (pseudodementia) is the commonest reversible cause of dementia. This has prognostic, therapeutic and, of course, social implications.

8. Acute confusional states (say due to infections, cardiac failure, medications etc.) may be super-imposed on an established dementia.

9. The main reasons for using imaging techniques (MRI or CT of the brain) are

a. to exclude any structural cause (meningioma, chronic subdural haematoma etc.) and

b. to know whether cortical or subcortical vascular disease are present.

10. Management:

a. Drugs – Donepezil and Rivastigmine are now available for the symptomatic treatment of mild to moderate Alzheimer's dementia. Co-ordination between GPs, Pyschiatrists, Neurologists and Geriatricians is essential for 'shared care'.

b. Non-drug management includes:

i. Discussing the diagnosis and plan of care with relatives and a multidisciplinary team.

ii. Giving information re: legal issues, e.g. Court of Protection to relatives.

iii. Putting the patient and carers in touch with social and other support services.

iv. Making the care-givers aware of the details of the Alzheimer's Disease Society (see below).

Final message

1. The diagnosis of Alzheimer's dementia is usually made by excluding other causes of dementia including reversible dementias. Thus, Alzheimer's dementia must be differentiated from at least three groups of conditions:

a. acute confusional states – they have rapid onset and symptoms fluctuate.

b. depression or pseudodementia, because depression causes loss of concentration. To complicate the matter further dementia itself leads to secondary depression and depression and dementia present concurrently as the disease manifests itself.

c. reversible causes of dementia (especially in those less than 60 years). The causes are alcoholism, B12 deficiency, hypothyroidism and normal pressure hydrocephalus.

2. More needs to be done for the overall management of Alzheimer's dementia: to continue research into (a) a specific drug based on understanding of molecular biology of Alzheimer's disease because on current indications the genetics of Alzheimer's disease is both complex and controversial, a specific drug is yet to be found; and (b) in improved Care in the Community.

Useful address

Alzheimer's Disease Society,
Gordon House,
10 Greencoat Place,
London SW1F 1PH
Tel: 0171 306 0606

(advice booklets available as a pack costing £4.00)

Appendix 1

Mini-Mental State Examination (adapted from Folstein *et al.*)

Patient name...

Date of birth .... Date of test ....

Section	Questions	Max. points	Patient score
1. Orientation	a) Can you tell me today's date/month/ year? Which day of the week is it today? Can you also tell me what season it is?	5	
	b) What city/town are we in? What is the county/country? What building are we in and on what floor?	5	
2. Registration	I should like to test your memory. (name 3 common objects: e.g. "ball, car, man")		
	Can you repeat the words I said? *(Score 1 point for each word)* (repeat up to 6 trials until all three are remembered) (record number of trials needed here:)	3	
3. Attention & Calculation	a) From 100 keep subtracting 7 and give each answer: stop after 5 answers. (93_86_79_72_65_).		

Section	Questions	Max. points	Patient score
	Alternatively **b)** Spell the word 'WORLD' backwards. (D_L_R_O_W).	5	
4. Recall	What were the three words I asked you to say earlier? *(Skip this test if all three objects were not remembered during registration test)*	3	
5. Language			
Naming	Name these objects (show a watch) (show a pencil)	2	
Repeating	Repeat the following: "no ifs, ands or buts"	1	
6. Reading	Show card or write ("CLOSE YOUR EYES")		
	Read this sentence and write what it says.	1	
Writing	Now can you write a short sentence for me?	1	
7. Three-stage	(Present paper)		
command	Take this paper in your left (or right) hand, fold it in half, and put it on the floor.	3	
8. Construction	Will you copy this drawing please?	1	
Total score		**30**	

Examiner...Notes..

Appendix 2

Main points of SMAC guidelines (i.e. guidelines by Standing Medical Advisory Committee)

1. Patients receiving Donepezil (Aricept) should be assessed after 12 weeks' treatment and should only continue on the drug if there is evidence of benefit.
2. Treatment should only be initiated and supervised by a specialist.
3. Specialists initiating treatment should ensure that patients selected for treatment are essentially the same as those described in published studies.
4. Further controlled trials are urgently needed to determine how long prescribing is justified for, even in patients who benefit initially.

References/Further reading list

1. Newsletter – European Health Promotion program on nutrition and Alzheimer's Disease. Number 1, 1998.

2. Developments in Alzheimer's disease by Cornelius Kelly in *Update for General Practitioners* – 18 March 1998 issue.

3. *Lectures Notes on Geriatrics*. Nicholas Coni and Stephen Webster, Fifth Edition, Blackwell Science Ltd, 1998

4. *Geriatric Medicine*. Vol 21, January 1998.

5. Dementia too costly to treat? *Health and Ageing*. June 1998 issue.

6. Pharmaco-genomics. *British Medical Journal*, Vol 316, 27 June 1998 issue.

Acknowledgement

I am extremely grateful to Professor Brice Pitt, Professor, Psychiatry of Old Age, at St Mary's Hospital Medical School, London for his help in preparing this chapter at its inception (during its first edition in 1994).

Parkinson's Disease

CHAPTER 11

I first remember coming into contact with a patient suffering from Parkinson's disease when I was about four – the patient was my next door neighbour. I, even now, vividly remember his fixed facial expression, stooped posture, short shuffling gait and saliva drooling from the angles of his mouth – the typical features of a patient with advanced Parkinson's Disease. In spite of this (or because of it!) he continued walking at least four miles every day until he was in his mid-seventies.

So what is Parkinson's disease?

It is a degenerative disorder and is due to changes in that part of the brain called substantia nigra with resulting reduction in a substance called Dopamine, giving rise to the symptoms and signs of the disease. Its cause is unknown – it is not a form of stroke or cancer but it usually affects people over the age of 60 and will affect one person in 100 of those over 65. There are several other conditions which give rise to Parkinson's-like symptoms, including encephalitis, repeated head injury through pursuits such as boxing, carbon monoxide poisoning and medical and neurological conditions such as severe depression and familiar tremors. Similar symptoms can also result as the side effects of drugs like Haloperidol, Maxolon and Largactil.

Symptoms and signs may vary, depending upon the stage of the illness, but three classical features of Parkinson's disease in variable combinations are:
1. bradykinesia *or* akinesia so that initiation of movement, dexterity and endurance become increasingly difficult. This is slow to develop.
2. rigidity of limbs.
3. Tremor of fingers which becomes much less obvious on voluntary movement.

In some patients only one half of the body is predominantly affected at first but patients may then start to develop a short shuffling gait, small handwriting and difficulty in maintaining proper posture and balance with a tendency to falling, sleep disorders, swallowing problems and constipation. Some patients later may also develop depression and confusional state with high risk of developing pressure sores.

Initially, especially in mild cases, diagnosis may pose problems in that there is no confirmatory laboratory or X-ray diagnosis.

In many patients only a therapeutic trial (trying the effect of the drug to see what happens to the symptoms, in this case Levodopa) either establishes *or* rules out the diagnosis of Parkinson's disease.

Brain scan (i.e. computed tomography of brain) and MRI scan (i.e. magnetic resonance imaging) may help only in sorting out the diagnosis of Parkinson's disease from other conditions which mimic it, otherwise they do not directly help in diagnosis.

A special scan of the brain called positron emission tomography (PET) may show loss of dopamine cells and pathways in Parkinson's but this may be expensive and is usually mainly a research procedure.

Drugs

Levodopa continues to be the most important drug for Parkinson's disease. It helps to replace dopamine and is available in conventional and controlled release form.

Patients in early stages may not need Levodopa. It is usually given when the symptoms interfere with activities of daily living (ADL), say when the patient has difficulty in walking. Dopamine receptor agonists are another group of drugs which are increasingly being added in treatment of Parkinson's disease in view of the long-term side effects of Levodopa. Drugs in this group include Pergolide, Ropinirole, Apomorphine and the little used Bromocriptine. This group of drugs may especially benefit younger patients from the point of view of long-term prognosis.

These agonists (drugs having a stimulating effect on certain cells in the brain as opposed to a replacement drug like Levodopa) are longer acting and free from long-term side effects, especially involuntary movements.

Apomorphine is given either by intermittent injection subcutaneously or by continuous subcutaneous infusion pump to those patients where other treatment is difficult to manage, and especially where there are marked fluctuations in the disease.

Apomorphine is a powerful drug of this class and can lead to marked improvement of the symptoms. It should be started under supervision and the use of an antiemetic (Domperidone) is advised as it can cause nausea

Tolcapone is a drug which has recently been marketed in the UK. It is a catechol-o-methyl transferase inhibitor. This leads to prolonged activity of Dopamine in the brain and hence its usefulness. Its efficacy is known to occur especially if it is used in conjunction with L-Dopa. The dose of L-Dopa should be reduced to 20 per cent when Tolcapone is added into the regime. Liver function test should be monitored. In view of its severe side effect on the liver, the licence of this drug has recently been suspended. However, a second drug of this class called Comtess (Entacapone) has recently been launched in the UK.

Other groups of drugs which are sometimes used in Parkinson's disease are Selegiline, anticholinergics (do not improve akinesia) and the anti-viral drug Amantadine which has a short-lived effect. It has rightly been suggested that management of patients with advanced Parkinson's disease requires far more than tinkering with drug regimes and, like many other chronic diseases, the need for a comprehensive approach to patient's management becomes paramount, more so in the later stage of the disease.

Surgical management in Parkinson's disease

After a lull of say a decade and half there is a resurgence of surgical procedures in managing

Parkison's disease. Surgery is helpful to only a small number of patients.

The three surgical procedures, since the mid-1980s:

1. Surgery on ventrolateral aspect of thalamus - thalamotomy – which helps tremor on the other side of the body but can also help rigidity, and to a limited extent, dyskinesias in a few patients.

2. Surgery in globus pallidus – pallidotomy. This surgical procedure is of proven value in dealing with dyskinesia and dystonia due to drugs.

3. Surgery in relation to subthalamic nucleus. Ablation of the nucleus is of considerable benefit especially with regard to akinesia, rigidity and tremor on the opposite side of the body.

The neurosurgeon has to be very careful with this operation in view of the technical problem with this procedure as the surrounding structures are quite close to this nucleus which in itself is a small vascular structure difficult to locate. Chorea is a possible risk of this operation.

4. Transplants which have some practical and ethical problems involve implantation of fetal nigral tissue and have been effective in few patients. Research is continuing to find other sources of dopaminergic tissue.

Rehabilitation

This is an important component of the overall management of Parkinson's disease and some general points need emphasising as these affect rehabilitation.

1. Rehabilitation for both elderly and young people is similar.

2. Elderly patients are not all the same and each one should be treated individually

and

3. The chances of a patient suffering from other diseases increase after 75 and consequently the number of drugs he or she will be taking. All in all, invaluable roles in rehabilitation are provided by the Physiotherapist who gives advice on posture, gait, balance; the Occupational Therapist who advises on aids to help with daily living and the Speech Therapist and Dietician who help with such areas as swallowing problems.

Recently a device made and launched by the Manufacturer Medtronic (Tel: 0181 938 3308) has shown to control rigidity, postural instability, bradykinesia and tremor of Parkinson's disease. This device called the activa system is implanted in the brain. The neurostimulator (consisting of battery and microelectric circuitry is placed under the skin near the collar bone) provides mild electrical stimulation which is carried to the electrodes implanted deep within the brain, i.e. in the subthalamic nucleus or globus pallidus. To turn the system on or off the patients use a hand held magnet (*Hospital Doctor* June 4, 1998).

Role of Social Services

The help of Social Services may be needed at various stages of the disease in the form of social help, sorting out benefits or accommodation needs (either intermittently in the form of respite care *or* permanent accommodation).

Role of Parkinson's disease Nurse Specialist

The Parkinson's disease Nurse Specialist helps with assessment of patients, their general management and initiation and supervision of Apomorphine treatment (both in the hospital and the community), she is also engaged in education.

Lastly, a word about the Parkinson's disease Society (PDS) which was formed in 1969.

PDS has 230 branches nationally. The PDS not only deals with the problems of patients and their relatives but is also engaged in providing information and research in Parkinson's disease.

Final message

1. The management of a patient with Parkinson's disease needs multidisciplinary input from the Specialist Consultant, other members of the rehabili-

tation team, Social Services, friends, relatives and other carers. This 'profound' illness affects them all and not only the patient.

2. The best advice which a patient with Parkinson's disease can be given is regarding keeping active and maintaining a positive attitude.

3. Management should include education and counselling. Besides, the wishes of the patients and carers should be taken into account at all stages of the patient's illness.

4. It is also essential that Hospital and General Practitioners maintain a good relationship for the 'shared care' of the patients and here the contribution by the Parkinson's disease Nurse Specialist is invaluable.

5. Further research – gene therapy – holds hope for improved treatment of Parkinson's disease in coming years.

Useful address

Parkinson's Disease Society
22 Upper Woburn Place,
London WC1H 0RA
Tel: 0171 383 3513

Further reading list/References

1. *Living with Parkinson's Disease*. This is a comprehensive information package for newly diagnosed people and their carers, from the Parkinson's Disease Society.

2. *Parkinson's Disease at your Fingertips* (by Marie Oxtoby and Adrian Williams), Class Publishing, London (1995).

3. *Guidelines for the Management of Parkinson's Disease* (by Parkinson's Disease Consensus Working Group), Hospital Medicine, June 1998.

4. Progress in treating Parkinson's Disease – Advances in Therapy – (by A. Manson and A. Lees) in *Update for General Practitioners*, 22 July, 1998 issue.

5. *Parkinson's Disease – a self help guide for patients and carers* (by M. Jahanshahi and D. Marsden *et al.*) Souvenir Press, ISBN 0-285 63317-1 (available from Books en route, P.O. Box 888, Wallington, Surrey, SM6 8PE. Price £14.99)

Booklet

1. An information booklet called *Moving On* is available from the Parkinson's Disease Society. The booklet offers advice and support regarding living day to day with Parkinson's Disease and its changing needs.

2. *Parkinson's Aware in Primary Care*: this is a guide for Primary Care Team. This publication has been produced mainly by General Practitioners for General Practitioners. Copies are available from Parkinson's Disease Society (see address above).

Members of Primary and Secondary Care Teams can also request a free copy of the publication entitled – *Pathways – a paradigm for disease management in Parkinson's Disease* – by sending a postcard with contact number and address to, Pathways Paradigm, P.O. Box 6, Hampton, Middlesex TW12 2HH.

Fits, Faints and Funny Turns

Abbreviation explained: E.E.G. = Electroencephalogram, i.e. 'tracing of brain-waves'

There is probably no other group of symptoms in medicine like fits, faints and funny turns for making a 'doctor's heart sink'. These symptoms are also variously described as dizziness, vertigo, collapses, blackouts, seizures and fits, syncope and lightheadedness. One 75-year-old lady even complained of 'dying four times yesterday'. Was she right? Well, yes, almost! More about this later in this article. To arrive at the correct diagnosis concerning these symptoms, a detailed history from the patient and an eye-witness are crucial. This should be followed by:

1. physical examination of the patient with special reference to examination of the cardiovascular system (heart and blood vessels) and brain.

2. investigations including blood tests, ECG (electrocardiogram) and if indicated, special scan of the brain, e.g. CT (computerised tomography), brain scan and even MRI (magnetic resonance imaging) of the brain. I will now discuss the main symptoms.

Syncope and Blackouts

Syncope is a sudden but transient loss of consciousness. There is loss of postural tone followed by a spontaneous recovery. Thus, a person starts feeling lightheaded, heaviness in legs, unsteadiness and a varying but brief period of unconsciousness with complete recovery. There are several causes of syncope. These include the 'common faint', especially common in young people, following prolonged standing, pain, emotional stress; postural hypotension (marked reduction in blood pressure on standing) found in many medical conditions and as a side effect of drugs. It may also be situational (cough, micturition and defaecation syncopes) and heart-rhythm disturbances. In fact, the lady mentioned above turned out to be suffering from heart block on 24 hour ECG monitor testing and was effectively treated by a pacemaker with complete cessation of her symptoms.

In this context two facts ought to be kept in mind:

1. In TIAs (transient ischaemic attacks, also called mini-strokes), syncope or blackouts are seldom a feature.

2. Prolonged confusion and sleepiness is not a feature of syncope. Think of seizures in such situations.

Vertigo: hallucinations of movement or 'dizziness'

Vertigo (remember watching James Stewart as a vertigo-afflicted police detective, in Alfred Hitchcock's 1958 film 'Vertigo', a downright peculiar thriller) is most likely due to problems in the balancing mechanisms in the inner ear, such as Meniere's disease or labyrinthitis, or to disease of the cerebellum (part of the brain concerned with co-ordination of posture, balance and fine voluntary movements) or its connections, from vertebrobasilar insufficiency, tumour, or multiple sclerosis. As is well known, vertigo is also found in travel sickness, fear of heights, anxiety and hyperventilation, alcohol use, anaemia and at times even epilepsy. Also, side effects of drugs are a possibility to be kept in mind. Vertigo or dizziness is not usually due to psychological causes *per se*.

...And what about the seizures?

So what leads to seizures? It results following a transient change in the way of working of cells of the brain. It is estimated that one in 130 people, i.e. approximately 420,000 people in the United Kingdom have epilepsy.

All jerking movements in the body are not necessarily due to epilepsy. Again, a history from an eye witness is of paramount importance (unfortunately an eye witness may not be available in the case of many elderly people having seizures, who incidentally are prone to have serious injury like fractured pelvis and even subdural haematoma). The history should include the circumstance of the episode, its duration, the frequency, posture of the patient, the time of occurrence, any injury (say tongue biting), urinary incontinence during the fits, unconsciousness (if so, for how long) and so on. Each of these give an important clue in reaching the diagnosis of seizure. History is thus the most important part of diagnosis. This is followed by examination of the patient and tests (blood tests, a routine chest X-ray, 24 hour ECG monitor and EEG). CT Brain Scan (or MRI scan) may be needed. Not everyone needs a scan though. It is however, prudent to rule out a brain tumour by a CT brain scan in a person aged 40 or above who has a fit for the first time.

It is very helpful to note that the two investigations (i.e. functional MRI and EEG) can now be performed simultaneously on a patient for the investigation of a seizure. This will help in further precision in management of epilepsy – both in diagnosis and treatment (drug treatment and if necessary, surgical treatment)

Causes and precipitating factors of seizures (at all ages)

A wide variety of conditions can trigger seizures. These include 'flickering lights' ('television epilepsy'), high fever (e.g. febrile convulsions in children), menstruation, alcohol abuse and extreme stress. Known causes of epilepsy include stroke (according to Oxford Community Stroke project findings, as reported in a recent British Medical Journal, there is 11.5 per cent risk of having single or recurrent fits during the first 5 years after stroke), hypoglycaemia (low blood sugar), head injury, meningitis, and not commonly, brain tumour. In 60 per cent of cases we do not know the cause of seizures (idiopathic epilepsy). However, in elderly patients most seizures usually have known causes. The seizures (epilepsy) may occasionally present as a syncope. One should recognise the possibility of 'pseudo-seizures' (i.e. non-epileptic seizures) especially in younger women with social, psychiatric and even sexual problems.

Finally, to diagnose epilepsy with certainty the seizures must be recurrent.

Management of fits, faints and funny turns

Management clearly depends on the cause. These include pacemaker implantation in patients with a heart block, valve replacement in those with aortic valve stenosis, treatment of meningitis *or* operation of a brain tumour and evacuating a subdural haematoma, where indicated. Patients with idiopathic epilepsy need long-term treatment with drugs. Single seizures do not necessarily need treatment. Several drugs are available such as Sodium Valproate (Epilim), Carbamazepine, Phenytoin, Lamotrigine, Gabapentin and others. The patients do need supervision and follow up. Effort should be made to control seizures by one drug. Blood levels of drug may need monitoring. Patients need advice concerning driving, jobs and a full explanation of their condition. Help and support from social services may be needed. Surgery may be considered in only selected, mainly younger, patients whose epilepsy is poorly controlled by drugs. There are only a few specialist centres to undertake this procedure. The management of epilepsy does not end with prescribing of drugs. Several other factors have to be considered and indeed discussed with both the patient and the family members. These include driving-implications, employment situation, patient's interests and social activities, family history of epilepsy and genetic implications, general safety precautions and although out of context, the risk of foetal malformation during pregnancy due to taking of anti-epileptic drugs. Also, epileptic patients who do not respond well to drug treatment may need to have a cardiological opinion as the diagnosis of epilepsy may be wrong. Indeed, misdiagnosis of epilepsy is a major clinical problem.

Future prospects in seizure-management

Our brain – the site of consciousness, language, emotions and information-processing – is the most complex organ in the body. Hence, in spite of considerable progress having been made during the last several decades in our understanding of functioning of the brain, there has been no proportionate progress either in preventing or in very successfully treating seizures.

Further research, e.g. (a) refinements in the classification of epilepsies and (b) new methods of focused drug-delivery (i.e. at the site of the brain which is the source of seizures), may be needed. All in all, we should continue to be optimistic regarding the future progress of seizures – there must be light at the end of the tunnel!

Final Message

1. The cornerstone of precise diagnosis of diseases presenting with fits, faints and funny turns, is a careful detailed history from the patient and the eyewitness. There should be no shortcut in this.

2. In view of occasional diagnostic uncertainties in the diagnosis of seizures (not to mention its consequent medico-legal and social implications), a second opinion may be required. Happily, advances in diagnosis and management of seizures are continuing.

3. Patients suffering from seizures (epilepsy) need and deserve explanation, information (backed by booklets), sensitivity and reassurance.

Useful adresses

The British Epilepsy Association
Anstey House,
40 Hanover Square,
Leeds LS3 1BE.
Tel: 0113 243 9393

The Epilepsy Association of Scotland
48 Govan Road,
Glasgow,
GSL 1JL.
Tel: 0141 427 4911

Further reading list:

1. *Epilepsy and Everyone* A British Epilepsy Association Publication (see address, above)

2. *The Encyclopedia of Epilepsy* (1997) edited by Prof. David Chadwick – Roby Education Limited.

3. *How the Mind Works* by Professor Steven Pinker (for general reading only)

4. *Managing Epilepsy in Primary Care* by Malcolm P. Taylor, Blackwell Science. ISBN 0 865 429723

Managing Osteoporosis

Osteoporosis is very common. It is a disease mainly affecting elderly females. Overall, more than 1 in 3 women and 1 in 12 men are affected. It costs the NHS over £940 million yearly to treat osteoporosis and related problems. (Out of a total of 200,000 fractures annually, 60,000 are hip fractures, mostly in the elderly). Osteoporosis affects bones, which are not dead tissues, but dynamic, being constantly replaced and remodelled. Osteoporosis, a major cause of illness and death of elderly people in this country, is characterised by low bone mass and the bones, especially of the hips, wrist and spine, are prone to fracture. Although the bone is weak, its various constituents are normal. The reduction of bone mass – usually occurring after 35 years (at this stage bone mass reaches its peak) is gradual and is 1 per cent per year in post-menopausal women, so much so that by the age of 80, women may have lost approximately 30 per cent of their initial bone mass and men up to 10 per cent. (1)

But why is osteoporosis mainly a female problem?

The reasons are:

1. Lower maximum bone development in women.
2. Menopausal effect.
3. There is prolonged life expectancy in females and hence there is a prolonged period of bone loss.

Happily, today, not only doctors, but the general public are becoming more and more aware that failure of the function of the ovary after the menopause results in osteoporosis and that a considerable degree of bone loss can be prevented by hormone replacement therapy. Clearly, it would be the height of ignorance to accept in this day and age that fractures are the natural consequences of ageing and that nothing could be done about it. But who are the would be osteoporosis sufferers?

Potentiating or risk factors

Apart from hormonal changes at the time of menopause and prolonged life expectancy of females as mentioned above, there are several other factors potentiating osteoporosis. These are:

1. If maximum bone mass is not attained during childhood and early adult life.
2. Evidence is now emerging of possible loss of bone mass (and consequent added risk of fracture

after menopause) in those women in whom there is even minimal disturbance of menstrual cycles. Efforts, therefore, should be made not only to increase peak bone mass, but also to preserve it as long as possible, before the menopause. (3)

3. Poor nutrition including poor calcium-intake (a diet rich in calcium, say milk, should be encouraged from childhood).

4. Family history of osteoporosis, especially those who are tall, slender and fair.

5. Medications – those who are taking certain drugs (steroids, for example).

6. Poor mobility and lack of exercise (activity leads to strong bones and vice versa).

7. Smoking and excessive alcohol intake predispose to osteoporosis.

Diagnosing osteoporosis

During the last 15 years bone mineral measurement has given an added momentum into osteoporosis research and management. Several techniques are available. These include single and dual photon absorptiometry (SPA and DPA), dual energy X-ray absorptiometry (DEXA) and quantitative computed tomography (QCT). During the last decade, there has been development of DPA into dual energy X-ray source, i.e. DEXA. Presently, it is being used widely. It is faster and produces results with good precision – as little as 1–3 per cent of the bone loss can be detected. These procedures have paved the way for early therapeutic intervention in osteoporosis. It is not suggested, however, that measurement of bone density will forecast future fractures with great accuracy as there are other factors in the equation.

It is universally accepted that the conventional X-ray to diagnose osteoporosis is too late in the day. In fact, there is a loss of between 30 and 50 per cent of bone mass by the time osteoporosis is diagnosed by conventional X-rays. Equally, the biochemical parameters are at present neither widely considered very helpful nor are they used widely

to diagnose osteoporosis. A few enthusiasts, however, are hopeful that this method would gain widespread acceptance in future.

Managing postmenopausal osteoporosis by HRT (hormone replacement therapy)

On current indications, for the prevention of osteoporosis, oestrogens are the treatment of choice.

1. To start with, women at risk of developing osteoporosis should be identified say on the basis of body build (tall, slender), family history of osteoporosis, ovarian function (menstrual disturbances or ovary taken out for medical reasons).

2. Before considering HRT, it is very important that women be offered full medical and gynaecological examination, including smear test and that they are made aware of the advantages and side effects (both short term and long term) of HRT. It must be realised that successful long-term treatment is possible only when both the doctor and woman want it. Compliance with HRT is poor.

3. Hormone replacement therapy should not be given to women with past or present breast or uterine cancer, history of jaundice of pregnancy, liver disease and thrombo-embolic diseases.

4. There is as yet no consensus over the duration of treatment, but even say, 10 years of treatment is unlikely to be fully protective (see below).

5. Oestrogen can be used in the form of tablets, patches or implants. The side effects on regular 'period' following treatment has been over-emphasized. However, new preparations of oestrogen and progesterone could be given continuously without causing vaginal bleeding. Also, the risk of developing cancer of the uterus by this long-term therapy with combined preparations of oestrogen and progesterone is substantially decreased.

6. The treatment helps to arrest postmenopausal bone loss ideally in early postmenopause, say in the fifties, but there is no reason why it cannot be given to those in their sixties or even seventies, with reasonable benefit. Indeed, it should be con-

tinued indefinitely because bone density and fracture risk 10 years after it had been stopped, are identical in women who had taken it and those who had not taken it.

Management of osteoporosis (see also Appendix 1)

Established osteoporosis
It is generally assumed that once a patient has established osteoporosis, nothing much can be done about it. In fact, a lot could be done to prevent further pain and disability. No doubt the therapeutic options are limited at this stage and the main emphasis is on symptomatic management and long-term care of the patient. (4) These are:

1. All environmental hazards (poor lighting, loose carpets and unstable furniture, etc.) that increase the risk of falling should be seen to. After all, in a patient with osteoporosis it is the injury (trauma) however trivial, which may give rise to fractures. (Please see Chapter 14 on Falls).

2. Hip fracture should be treated with internal fixation and early mobilisation should be encouraged. In view of possible complications, the early mobilisation is so important that a very famous orthopaedic surgeon, now retired, commented that one ought to change one's orthopaedic surgeon if a patient is unable to mobilise 48 hours after hip surgery !

3. Of course, not all patients are fit for surgery after a hip fracture. Some will need adequate pain-control and a period of immobilisation to give time for healing of fracture.

4. Prolonged use of corsets for patients with osteoporotic fractures of vertebrae is not recommended. It gives a false sense of security and indeed is a positive hindrance regarding their mobility. The corset, if used at all, should be given only for a limited period, i.e during the acute pain stage.

5. Geriatricians have a great role in helping orthopaedic surgeons in the management of elderly hip-fracture patients – both before and after operations. Indeed, nationwide, there is a large gap between what is being done at present and what actually needs to be done. Earlier involvement of geriatricians in the management of such patients is long overdue.

6. Calcium in large doses can help by decreasing bone loss in patients over 35 years. Combined Calcium and vitamin D preparations should be considered in those aged 75 years, especially those who are housebound, (Cacit D3, 1–2 sachets daily; Calcichew D3 Forte, 2 tablets daily, Calceos 1 tablet twice daily.)

7. *Prevention of falls* is one of the most important measures in preventing hip fracture. Sensible use of drugs and environmental modifications should be aimed at. Use of hip protectors, especially in Nursing Homes residents, should be considered.

8. *Exercise*. Weight bearing exercises like brisk walking, running and playing tennis are clearly not suitable for frail, elderly women. Nevertheless, they should be encouraged to be more mobile and active.

9. The use of thiazide diuretics is known to reduce the risk of hip fracture.

10. Apart from HRT, bisphosphonates are being used in treatment of postmenopausal osteoporosis. The two bisphosphonates used are:

a. Cyclical therapy with etidronate disodium (Didronel PMO) for 5 years or beyond and

b. Alendronic acid (Fosamax). Fosamax should be used with caution in patients with upper gastro-intestinal problems, e.g. gastritis and oesophageal problems.

11. Subcutaneous salcatonin in doses of 100 IU daily is useful in osteoporosis and is effective in severe pain due to vertebral fractures. It is costly though.

Corticosteroid induced osteoporosis
Steroids have been used for 40 years or so and have revolutionised the management of several medical

conditions: asthma, rheumatoid arthritis, some skin diseases and bowel problems like ulcerative colitis and others. However, high doses of these drugs have also been responsible for causing thinning of bones, i.e. osteoporosis and osteoporotic fractures. Studies show that only 14 per cent of the patients have been given preventive treatment for osteoporosis. Failure to prevent/treat steroid-induced osteoporosis may have medico-legal implication.

So who is at risk?

Patients receiving more than 7.5 mg of Prednisolone daily for 6 months or more (though the effect may start after several week's of steroid treatment).

What needs to be done?

Measures include:

1. making patients aware of this side effect – this is a doctor's ethical, medical and legal responsibility.

2. reducing the dose of Prednisolone, preferably below 7.5 mg daily, if possible.

3. Before considering treatment to prevent or treat steroid-induced osteoporosis, diagnosis needs to be made by measuring bone density by DEXA scan.

4. for postmenopausal women HRT should be considered. If it is inappropriate, bisphosphonate for example etidronate; and testosterone in men, should be given.

5. A drug called Deflazacort can be given instead of Prednisolone. Deflazacort has a bone-sparing effect and can be regarded as a bone friendly corticosteroid. It is costly though.

6. In some situations, to reduce the risk of osteoporosis, high doses of 'booster' doses of steroids for a short time (days or weeks) are given instead of long-term oral treatment.

Male osteoporosis

This subject has received attention only recently. Osteoporosis affects 1 in 12 men in this country. In half of the cases, the causes are unknown. Hypogonadism, steroid use, alcohol abuse and even cancer are known causes. Once again, diagnosis should be confirmed by measurement of bone mass by densitometry. Treatment by testosterone in those who have hypogonadism is clearly very effective but symptomatic treatment for pain (e.g. when there is fracture, say vertebrae) with painkillers, transcutaneous electrical nerve stimulation and physiotherapy, should be given. As prevention is better than cure, every effort should be made to prevent falls.

Need for District osteoporotic service

Every District General Hospital in the country needs an osteoporosis service. For this to function adequately, provision of Bone Densitometry is essential. By offering preventive treatment with HRT, there should be a considerable drop in the number of fractures in the future, in the group of patients with the least bone mass. On balance, widespread general screening for osteoporosis is unlikely to be cost-effective. At any rate, apart from diagnosing osteoporosis, monitoring the effect of treatment and research are other uses of bone densitometry.

(For European Community's recent recommendations on osteoporosis please see Appendix 2 at the end of this chapter).

Final message

1. In most cases, osteoporosis can be prevented and treated. Encouraging a healthy lifestyle at all ages is paramount.

2. Happily, regular meetings and symposia are now taking place – both in this country (Bath, for example) and outside (e.g. Copenhagen, Denmark) where epidemiologists, endocrinologists, geriatricians, rheumatologists and other physicians, gynaecologists and others present and discuss osteoporosis-related research and, of course, management of osteoporosis.

3. It is not a disease exclusively of old age, but can be found in patients of all age-groups.

4. New drug treatments of this disabling disorder have improved the management.

Useful address

The National Osteoporosis Society (N.O.S.)
P.O. Box 10,
Radstock,
Bath BA3 3YB.
Tel 01761 471771
Helpline: 01761 472 721

[National Osteoporosis Society is an independent and unbiased organisation. It gives help and information on osteoporosis and research related to it. It has lobbied the Government and Health Authorities and has transformed awareness of osteoporosis in the U.K. in the last 10 years.]

References/Further reading list

1. *Lecture notes in Geriatrics* (Coni and Webster) 5th Edition, (1998) Blackwell Science.

2. 'Pre-menopausal bone loss – a risk factor for osteoporosis', *New England Journal of Medicine*, 1990, 323: 1271-72.

3. *Post-menopausal Osteoporosis – The Silent Epidemic.* National Osteoporosis Society and European Foundation for Osteoporosis and Bone Disease, 1990.

4. 'Osteoporosis', *Medicine International*, 22: 5, May 1994, pp. 209–12.

5. *Hospital Doctor,* September, 13 1990.

6. 'Give bones a higher priority,' *Health Care Management,* Vol. 2, April 1994, pp. 43–44.

7. *Building Strong Bones and Preventing Fracture –* Summary Report on Osteoporosis in the European Community. European Communities/European Foundation for Osteoporosis 1998.

8. Advance reports – osteoporosis in men. *Geriatric Medicine*, Vol. 27, July 1997 issue, Page 23.

9. Hormone Replacement Therapy by Elizabeth Barrett-Connor in *British Medical Journal* Vol 317; 15 August 1998 issue (Page 457–61)

10. Medico-political Digest: *British Medical Journal*, 5 December, 1998, page 1598.

Booklets (all published by National Osteoporosis Society)
1. Osteoporosis
2. Osteoporosis in Men
3. Corticosteroids and Bone
4. Breast cancer and HRT
5. Treatments
6. Exercise and Physiotherapy

Appendix 1

Osteoporosis: Patient Profile

Name

Age

A. Symptoms:

B. History:

Life-style/exercise/occupation

Diet

Medications (mainly steroids?)

Positive family history of osteoporosis?

Oophorectomy (age)?

Gastrectomy?

Excessive drinking of alcohol?

Smoking?

C. Examination

Mobility

Weight

Body build

Clinical evidence of osteoporosis, i.e. back pain due to fracture, dorsal kyphosis

Blood pressure

Other symptoms

D. Investigations

Chest X-ray

Spine X-ray (lateral lumbar spine)

Full blood count

Serum Ca./Phos/Alk. Phos.

Others

• Bone densitometry

E. Management – Advice re:

• Drugs – analgesics, bisphosphonates, hormone replacement therapy in some.

F. General advice re:

1. Diet

2. Exercise

3. Fall prevention measures (assess re. postural hypotension, cataract, foot problems, dealing with environmental hazards, and consider use of hip protectors (especially in nursing-home residents)

4. Other measures

Appendix 2

Abbreviation explained: EC = European Community)

Key recommendations on Osteoporosis

- Adopt osteoporosis as a major health-care priority and initiate health promotion campaigns
- Establish co-ordinated systems for monitoring fracture rates at both national and EC levels
- Co-ordinate national systems to plan for expected increased demands on care of osteoporosis patients
- Advise the public and health-care professionals about the importance of calcium, vitamin D and exercise in fighting osteoporosis
- Make bone density measurements accessible and reimbursible – for individuals at high risk
- Develop co-ordinated guidelines in criteria for standard treatment strategies
- Provide financial support to national patient and scientific societies
- Fund additional research in key areas of prevention and treatment

[Source: *Osteoporosis Review* July 1998 Vol. 6 (National Osteoporosis Society) (Full text of the Study and 'Report on osteoporosis in the European Community – Action for Prevention' is available from the European Foundation for Osteoporosis. Fax 33472 369052)]

Falls and the Elderly

CHAPTER 14

Starting with a brief introduction, this chapter enumerates the causes of falls and then fall-preventing strategies. This is followed by a summary. The chapter ends by giving a résumé of audit points in elderly fallers.

Introduction

Nobody will deny the fact that good mobility is one of the essential ingredients of activities of daily living and hence a pre-requisite for independent life. It is not suprising, therefore, that after a fall, a person feels that independence is slipping away. This becomes more important in the elderly whose independence is likely to be affected also by other problems. Falls are one of the four most common problems in elderly patients; others are immobility, urinary incontinence and dementia. A fall, like a headache, should be considered as a symptom and not a disease. There are several causes of falls.

The incidence of falls rises with age and fracture of a bone is its important complication.

It is *twice as common in women as men;* 20 per cent of men and 40 per cent of women living at home had a history of fall during previous months.

Causes of falls

There are numerous causes of falls including,

1. *Physical*	- arthritis
	- Parkinson's disease
	- foot problems
	- strokes
	- cardiac failure
	- cardiac arrhythmias i.e. heart-rhythm abnormalities
2. *Mental*	- depression
	- dementia
3. *Drugs/ medications*	- sedatives (sleeping tablets)
	- diuretics (water tablets)
	- hypotensive agents (drugs which lower blood pressure)

4.	*Environmental factors*	- hazards in the home (rugs, mats, loose carpets, poor lighting, cluttered furniture).
		- inclement weather conditions (high wind/ice)
5.	*Age-related changes*	- balance/gait abnormalities
		- general frailty
		- poor vision
		- poor mobility

In only 16 per cent of cases was no cause found.

(Note: For the audit of falls in an elderly population, see appendix at the end of this chapter.)

Some practical steps to prevent falls

Postural hypotension

This condition needs to be suspected, recognised and hence falls prevented. Many patients experience a sensation of giddiness, mainly during a rapid change of posture such as standing quickly from a lying or even a sitting position.

This change in blood pressure with posture (postural hypotension) is significant when either there is fall in systolic blood pressure; (measured in lying and standing positions), of 20 mm of mercury or a fall of 10 mm of mercury in diastolic blood pressure. This definition is arbitrary.

Why does this happen? The problem may be partly due to an ageing autonomic nervous system, (i.e. failure of arterial baroreflex, most commonly due to disorders of the autonomic nervous system). However, some cases are undoubtedly triggered by taking drugs, for example, diuretics for the treatment of hypertension or cardiac failure, drugs used in Parkinson's Disease, in depression, and sleeping tablets. It is worth emphasising that the side effects of drugs are more common in the elderly. The reason?

This is not only due to reduced drug metabolism and decreased drug clearance but also because of the frequent need for multiple drug therapy. Patients with postural hypotension should be asked to change their posture gradually. Their medications need complete review, including reduction or stoppage.

Some patients with recurring symptoms may benefit by wearing elastic stockings, elevation of the head end of the bed during the night. Drug therapy includes fludrocortisone, midodrine and desmopressin. Of course, these drugs may give rise to side effects as well.

What else can be done?

Identify at risk group Those over 75 years, housebound and with obvious balance problems should be carefully monitored and even investigated.

Beware of multiple causes in a patient For example, vertebro-basilar insufficiency (VBI), secondary to arthritis of the back of the neck as the sole cause of falls in the elderly, is an over-diagnosed condition. This may lead to unwarranted complacency on the part of the clinician.

I vividly remember a patient of mine who fell frequently due to complete heart block (the patient subsequently had a cardiac pacemaker and had no further falls), but was initially thought to have the above diagnosis, i.e. VBI; therefore it is important to arrange 24 hour holter recording in these patients to rule out heart rhythm abnormalities.

A comprehensive assessment of the patient after a fall

This includes full clinical examination, preceded by an accurate history of the circumstances leading to a fall or falls. Important clues to the diagnosis can be found by observing the patient's gait, (e.g. in stroke), peripheral neuropathy, arthritis etc. or feet (e.g. infection, ulcer, ingrowing toe nails or even ischaemia).

This should follow relevant investigations, and management will depend on the problems detected.

It should take into account drug side effects, including postural hypotension as discussed above.

Many falls are preventable

An occupational therapist after a home visit will identify the environmental causes of falls, i.e. loose carpets, cluttered or unsuitable pieces of furniture (two patients with previous strokes used rocking chairs!).

Patients whose main cause of fall is poor balance, may be helped by balance exercises as offered by Physiotherapists.

Correction of vision in patients with poor sight will clearly be of considerable help.

Simple explanation and education rather than drugs are needed in some situations. For example, prescribing the anti-nausea drug, Stemetil, (prochlorperazine) to patients with giddiness (which may well be due to age-related balance problems) is not only unnecessary but is also dangerous, as this may cause many side effects, including postural hypotension and falls.

Hip protectors (a plastic shield sewn into special underwear so that it lies over the greater trochanter) are known to absorb energy when a patient falls, thus reducing the incidence of hip fractures. They are especially beneficial in patients who live in residential and nursing homes, who are very frail and hence have thin bones and are prone to recurrent falls and fractures.

Unfortunately compliance with these aids is poor at the present time.

Before a patient with fall is discharged from hospital, he or she must be instructed how to get up again after a fall

Identifying the cause of falls may not be enough because some patients who have fallen are liable to fall again as they develop a dread of further falls which may present as a pathological phobia. This group of patients may need repeated reassurances and be encouraged to keep active regardless.

Summary

1. Treatment of obvious causes of falls, stopping the offending drugs and overall improvement in general health of the patient are the initial management strategies in the care of a patient with a fall.

2. We should encourage elderly patients, especially those under 75, to be more active and have exercise, directed mainly at maintaining good balance.

3. One should also take advantage of various technological advances, i.e. portable alarm systems to summon help to a falling patient.

4. Regular follow up of the 'at risk' groups could be monitored by the geriatric health visiting team/district nurses.

5. A computerised list of 'at risk' groups of patients maintained by GPs is of considerable help to health visitors.

6. It is heartening to note that researches in mechanisms of falls and balance disorders are being carried out at various centres, both in this country and abroad.

7. More importantly however, as a practical help now, regular assessment of patients aged 75 and above by GPs will go a long way to preventing many patients from falling.

Final message

1. Causes of falls are usually multifactorial.

2. Many causes of falls are preventable by a comprehensive programme (by multidisciplinary involvement) by stopping medications where necessary, by removing hazards at home, providing rehabilitation including balance exercises and even by behaviour modification.

3. Research into the causes of falls needs to be expanded and continued.

References/Further reading list

1. *Dizziness & Balance Problems – A Guide to Causes and Treatments* – British Brain and Spine Foundation, ISBN 1 901893 02 2.

2. Orthostatic hypotension in the elderly: aetiology, manifestations and management (by Aparajit B. Dey, Rose Anne Kelley) in *Journal of the Irish Colleges of Physicians and Surgeons* Vol 27, July 1998: 182–187

3. *Falls in the Elderly*, by Joanna H. Downton Edward Arnold (1993). Paperback

4. Medical Progress – Injury prevention - by F. P. Rivara *et al.* in *The New England Journal of Medicine*, August 28, 1997: 613–618

Appendix

(abbreviation explained: MI = Myocardial infarction, i.e. Heart attack; GIT = Gastrointestinal tract)

Audit of geriatric falls

1. Date of observation ....

2. Patient's details:

    Name: ....

    Age: ....

    Sex: ....

3. No. of falls during the last year ....

4. Is balance (general frailty) a problem .... Yes/No

5. Cognitive impairment? .... Yes/No (if yes, its extent)

6. Active illness (infection,GIT haemorrhage, etc)? .... Yes/No

7. Cardiac causes (arrhythmias, MI etc)?... Yes/No

8. Arthritis? .... Yes/No

9. Parkinson's Disease?... Yes/No

10. Stroke/TIA? .... Yes/No

11. Alcohol abuse .... Yes/No

12. Drugs:

    (a) sleeping tablets .... Yes/No

    (b) drugs causing postural hypotension?... Yes/No

13. Vision: (Please tick relevant line)

Normal _____

Mildly impaired _____

Vision severely affected including blindness (one or both eyes) _____

14. Environment: (please ring one)

Inside: - Stairs - Carpet - Bathroom - Lighting - Others (including pets) ....

Outside: - Ice - Wind - Road traffic accidents ....

15. Other relevant comments ....

....

....

Preventive Care for the Elderly

"The first imperative for those wishing to be a healthy hundred is to be informed, to stay in command, and to be thoroughly obstreperous in refusing to be fobbed off with second-rate care".

- J. Grimley-Evans 1994

Aches and Pains, Pins and Needles

CHAPTER 15

Aches and pains, and pins and needles are common symptoms, especially the former. Pain is a very complex human experience. It is no wonder then, that patients vary their choice of words to describe these symptoms. They, for example, are known to describe their severe agonising pain as 'sort of ache', muscle pain as 'weak muscles' and pins and needles simply as 'pain' or vice versa. It may well be that their thinking is dependent on their perception of the cause of the symptom. Pain may be mild or severe. Apart from its physical component, severity of pain is also dependent on cultural and psychological factors. Strong emotions are known to override pain signals from the body – the classical example given is that of a soldier who fights on, not caring for his injuries.

Pain may be acute or chronic. While acute pain helps in arriving at its diagnosis, the 'function' of chronic pain is rather blurred. It is not surprising, therefore, that the pain-sufferer may have to look for its relief by different professionals. Several medical conditions (these include arthritis, 'trigeminal' neuralgia which is an exquisitely painful stabbing sensation down one side of the face; post-herpetic neuralgia i.e. persistent neuralgic pain felt in an area previously affected by shingles; back problems, bed sores, pain following immobility such as stroke and other medical conditions; and ischaemic legs, i.e. pain following inadequate blood supply) give rise to chronic i.e. longstanding pain. As an understanding of the mechanisms of pain has evolved, so has the management-

approach: from simple pain-killers such as paracetamol to more specific classes of drugs, radiotherapy and even surgery. In this article only medical conditions with longstanding pain, mainly due to involvement of muscles and nerve have been described:

Aches and pains – where predominantly muscles are involved

It is a common knowledge that aches and pains follow unaccustomed exercise, say jogging or cycling. This sort of 'ache' is self-limiting. Marathon runners are known to develop severe muscle pain. They may need help in the form of physiotherapy, painkillers and, of course, a brief rest. The maxim, no pain, no gain - the enduring of physical exercise – holds no water. The acute muscle pain due to viral illness (e.g. influenza virus and less commonly coxsackie virus) also respond to pain-killers and rest. In 'fibrositis', however, involvement of muscles and connective tissue gives rise to tenderness of muscles with poor sleep and even depression. These patients – some of them may have protracted symptoms – benefit from antidepressants, e.g. Amitriptyline and simple analgesics (paracetamol, for example).

Muscle cramps

These are also called 'muscle spasms'. This follows involuntary contraction of a muscle or group of muscles. This may be found in the following situations/medical conditions:-

1. following exercise including swimming
2. in kidney failure
3. in pregnancy (mentioned here for the sake of completeness)
4. hypothyroidism
5. in states or conditions with electrolyte imbalance e.g. following fluid-loss from the body (e.g. diarrhoea *or* excessive sweating in a very warm environment)
6. nocturnal cramps – classically manifest by flexion of toes and ankles. These patients are helped by medications like quinine *or* even drugs used in epilepsy such as Phenytoin *or* Carbamazepine.

Tetany

Here a patient develops carpo-pedal spasm (i.e. spasms of the muscle of hands and feet). This is due to involvement of peripheral nerves. Treatment is by correction of body's calcium, magnesium *or* acid–base derangement.

Polymyalgia rheumatica

Here patients, usually over 60 years of age, have stiffness and pain in both shoulders and adjoining areas. The ESR (erythrocyte sedimentation rate) is raised. Treatment with steroids is very effective.

The dose of steroids e.g. Prednisolone, should be reduced gradually in, say 4 to 6 week's time, to minimum possible dose (5 to 7.5 mg prednisolone daily approx.) which is in keeping with patient's symptoms and the ESR within normal limits. Steroids should be continued for about 2 years.

Chronic fatigue syndrome

Also called ME or myalgic encephalomyelitis, there is protracted fatigue after a whole range of illnesses. The symptoms are non-specific (e.g. muscle tenderness, weakness, fatigue and low grade fever). Viral illness should be ruled out by appropriate tests. Indeed, other medical conditions with similar symptoms, should be ruled out before the patient is given this diagnostic label. This condition affects people of all ages. There is no diagnostic test or a recognised treatment. Many patients are offered continued psychological counselling.

Drug side-effect or withdrawal causing aches and pains

Several drugs may give rise to muscle ache and pain with weakness, as their side effects. The drugs include steroids, Bumetanide, Chloroquine, Lithium and Isoniazide and Statins (drugs which lower cholesterol in the blood). Reduction in the doses, or if necessary (or possible) stopping the drug should be considered. Sudden withdrawal of certain anti-depressants may give rise to numbness and a sensation of electric shock.

Pins and needles (where nerves or their contral connections are predominantly involved)

'Pins and needles' may be a feature of several medical conditions. They include TIAs (transient ischaemic attacks) or mini-strokes, multiple sclerosis, peripheral neuropathies and other medical conditions where nerves are affected, infiltrated or trapped, e.g. cancers, cervical and or lumbar spondylosis, post-herpetic neuralgia and also central neurogenic pain.

Post-herpetic neuralgia (neuralgia is nerve pain)
In this condition the pain usually starts a month after the healing of the rashes of shingles. Seventy five per cent of the patients are over 60 years of age. Amitriptyline (an antidepressant) is a useful drug to use but there is an interval of some weeks before the patients get relief from neuralgic pain. If necessary, other measures to treat severe neuralgic pain are taken (see below).

Central neuralgic pain
About 1–2 per cent of stroke sufferers have spontaneous central (arising in brain) pain. This has been called 'thalamic' syndrome in the past. The thalamus, in fact, is not affected directly in all cases but in pathways leading to or from the thalamus. The condition now is called 'Central Post-Stroke Pain' (CPSP) Apart from classical stroke, this condition thus may be found in surgically treated subarachnoid haemorrhage, tumour removal and head injury. The patients are usually younger than average 'stroke' patients and weakness due to stroke is not severe. The pain may start *soon* after the stroke is complete, or comes on up to 18 months after stroke, when the pain may have 'burning', shooting, *or* even 'indescribable' character, brought about by movement. There is no pain if the patient is completely still. Pain intensity varies – like 'pins and needles' or excruciating. There is almost always deficit of temperature sensation. Early treatment is advised. Management includes:
• Medical – Amitriptyline and anticonvulsants (i.e. drugs used in epilepsy)
• TENS (transcutaneous electrical nerve stimulation which is treating long-persistent pain by passing small electrical currents into the spinal cord or sensory nerves by means of electrodes applied to skin)
• Surgical – peripheral sympathetic blockage, where feasible.

Peripheral neuropathies
There are several causes, e.g. diabetes, alcohol abuse, various cancers and drug side effects. Diabetic neuropathy is the most common cause of neuropathy. It is present without pain in most diabetic patients. If pain is present, it can be distressing. Management includes:
• tight control of diabetes, often with insulin
• anti-depressant (Amitriptyline is very helpful for night pain which is usually burning in character)
• for day time 'shooting pain', Phenytoin is helpful
• other measures: provision of sensible shoes, use of TENS machine.

Trigeminal neuralgia
Patients are usually middle aged or elderly (but trigeminal neuralgia may be an early feature of multiple sclerosis in young women). Pain comes on by activities like shaving, brushing the teeth, washing or even touching the face, cold exposure, eating *or* talking. Pain comes on in paroxysms and last for only a few seconds. Treatment is by Carbamazepine. As it is not a pain-killer, patients should not expect benefit for several days. If this does not help in full doses for up to a month, a neurosurgical referral should be considered as several surgical options are available. It is also important to differentiate this condition from 'atypical facial pain' which is usually considered psychogenic. This label, however, should be used only after carefully ruling out other causes of facial pain. Only then, treatment with pain-killers (such as paracetamol *or even* non-steroidal anti-inflammatory drugs) in conjunction with antidepressants (such as Amitriptyline) should be given and if necessary, the help of a Clinical Pyschologist *or* even a Psychiatrist sought.

Cancer pain (Please see chapter 17 on Management of Cancer in the Elderly)
It is an unpleasant sensory and emotional experience. A thorough history is essential. Investigations may be necessary to determine its cause/causes.

Some patients think that cancer-pain is inevitable and that strong pain-killers (e.g. Morphine group of drugs) are harmful. It is essential, therefore, that cause of pain and proposed treatment be explained to the patient. If there are bone metastases (i.e. spread of cancer to the bone), and spinal cord compression, radiotherapy is very helpful for pain relief. Surgery helps pain due to pathological (spread of cancer to bone) fracture of long bones. Other measures include general pain control. Here one should proceed slowly from simple pain-killers (i.e. Paracetamol) to Morphine. If drugs cannot be given by mouth, they should be given by injection including subcutaneous infusion of say, Diamorphine and Metoclopramide by portable syringe drivers. Besides, pain threshold may be raised by factors like disease knowledge and explanation (cause of pain may be cancer, radiotherapy, chemotherapy, or even other medical conditions like angina *or* arthritis), rest, sleep, reduction of anxiety, diversional activities, companionship, understanding, sympathy and hope.

Morphine-resistant pain

In pain due to nerve infiltration (including intractable post-herpetic neuralgic pain), one needs to use antidepressants (like Amitriptyline) with or without an anticonvulsant (such as Sodium Valproate) and steroids. If necessary, help and advice from the pain clinic should be sought.

General comments on management

1. It is thus clear from the above account that pain management depends on its cause/causes, severity and acuteness or chronicity. To this must be added the psychological and, where indicated, the cultural factors.

2. Non-steroidal – anti-inflammatory pain killers, steroids, anti-inflammatory drugs and even strong pain pain-killers, i.e. Morphine group of drugs, need to be used, if indicated. Where Morphine is needed to alleviate pain, it should be given as-and-when necessary basis in acute pain conditions. However, it should be given on a regular, fixed dose basis in chronic (long-standing) pain conditions.

3. Treatment of neuropathic pain (i.e. pain due to irritation or injury of peripheral nerves) in conditions like post-herpetic neuralgia, trigeminal neuralgia or diabetes with Amitriptyline should be prolonged and doses increased slowly.

4. Acupuncture does have some place in chronic pain conditions but the procedure needs to be repeated regularly for pain relief. Apart from acupuncture and TENS, measures like massage, relaxation, hypnotherapy and cognitive-behavioural therapy, have been used to treat longstanding persistent pain.

5. It is realised that cure is not possible in most patients with pain due to neuropathic conditions or cancer pain. However, patients do need support and adequate pain control. Members of a palliative care team from a London Hospital, have pointed out in a recent issue of the Journal of Royal College of Physicians of London, about the high level of inadequate symptom-control (pain being commonest) in hospital inpatients. This need not be so as adequate pain control is the doctor's/hospital palliative care team's paramount responsibility, especially in view of the availability of an armamentarium of pain-killers and other measures.

Final message

1. One should aim at adequate pain control, keeping in mind the physical, cultural and psychological aspects of pain and also the various options which are available for dealing with it.

2. Explaining to the patient the condition/conditions giving rise to pain, judicious use of certain anti-depressants (such as Amitriptyline) and involving hospital's palliative care team *or* Pain Clinics, makes the task of pain control much easier.

References/Further reading list

1. *Emergency Medicine Secrets* (Eds. Marcov-chick, Pons and Wolfe). Hanley and Belfus, Philadelphia, 1993.

2. *Oxford Textbook of Geriatric Medicine* (Eds. Grimley Evans and Franklin Williams). Oxford University Press, 1992.

3. *British Medical Bulletin* Vol 47; Churchill Livingstone, July, 1991.

4. Neuropathic pain by E. Charlton in *Prescriber's Journal*, Vol 33, 1993.

5. *Quantum healing* by Deepak Chopra; Bantam Books, June, 1990.

6. *A Guide to Care of the Elderly* (Eds. Shukla and Brooks), H.M.S.O. Books, 1996.

Cold Weather and the Elderly

[Abbreviations explained : E.C.G. = Electrocardiogram, E.E.G. = Electroencephalogram]

In the summer months we see a lot more smiling faces than in the winter months, probably because very few of us enjoy the discomfort cold weather brings. This is especially true of the elderly, particularly those who are housebound. But why are the elderly vulnerable to cold weather?

The adverse effect of cold on elderly people can be for various reasons: poor physical and mental health; inefficient body temperature regulating mechanism due to ageing; and poor living conditions.

In an average winter in England and Wales, about 40,000 more people die than in countries with a warmer climate.

It may surprise many that the deaths due to hypothermia form a tiny percentage of these deaths - about 1 per cent. Nevertheless, one should not under-estimate the seriousness of hypothermia and every effort should be made to lower the incidence. However, it is true to say that heart and lung problems (heart attack, pneumonia, bronchitis and stroke, etc.) caused by cold weather are a far greater danger to an elderly person's life than hypothermia.

In this chapter I shall, therefore, discuss the wider problems and the effects of cold weather on elderly people rather than hypothermia alone.

It is interesting to note that every year, especially during the winter months, there is wide reporting of hypothermia in various medical and non-medical journals and national newspapers, yet in even moderately cold conditions, the incidence of heart attacks and strokes increases because of the increased viscosity of blood and the narrowing of blood vessels, causing the blood pressure to rise.

It is known that improvements in housing in Finland and more central heating in New York (compared to London) have decreased the incidence of lung disease and ischaemic heart disease (i.e. angina and heart attacks) respectively. (Houses are colder in the U.K. than in U.S.A. generally).

At any rate, good home heating and insulating do increase one's comfort.

It is important to realise, however, that one should not be concerned only with the lower indoor temperature, as it is known that exposure to cold outside one's home is the major cause of mortality in the elderly.

The British tradition of fresh air and long walks should be curtailed during very cold winter weather. Adequate warm clothing, including woollen hats and gloves, should be worn, if such walks are unavoidable.

Hypothermia

In this condition the core body temperature is lower than 35°C and ideally this is recorded by a low reading thermometer. There may even be loss of consciousness.

Unless exposed to extremes of cold, younger people are protected from hypothermia because of their adequate body temperature regulating mechanism, good mobility and sensible clothing.

Hypothermia, therefore, is common in people who live alone and in those over 75 years old. Incidence of hypothermia is 10 per cent in elderly patients living at home and 4–34 per cent in those hospitalised.

It is a sad fact that the older one is, the poorer one is likely to be, and hence the ability to keep warm and be well nourished diminishes.

However, it should not be assumed that only an elderly person living on his or her own without central heating is likely to suffer from hypothermia in the middle of the winter months; it could occur even in summer, if an elderly person has, for instance, been lying on the floor for some reason say, following a fall or a stroke.

It could also occur after an operation, especially if a patient's bed is near an open window.

It is important to realise that most cases of hypothermia in elderly people are due to, or precipitated by acute medical problems, i.e. stroke, pneumonia etc. or diseases like hypothyroidism and cirrhosis of the liver and poor mobility. Many of them also happen to have poor nutrition.

The question then arises as to why the elderly are prone to hypothermia? Apart from age-related changes of defective body temperature regulation, the majority of those suffering from hypothermia after acute illness have been exposed to an unusually cold temperature. Their poor or non-existent mobility, diminished shivering, and associated confusion with consequent inability to fully understand as to where they are lying, hastens the onset of hypothermia.

The situation may be further compounded by medications like sleeping tablets or more commonly by tablets like Largactil (Chlorpromazine).

For the prevention of hypothermia a lot has already been said, i.e. the importance of keeping warm, having adequate nutrition and knowing one's financial rights. It is equally important that the acute medical conditions of elderly patients be treated urgently.

What else should be done? Every physician visiting an elderly patient at home should have a low reading thermometer. An electrocardiogram shows slow pulse rate, bradycardia and J waves. It should be the duty of the community as a whole to see that an elderly person at risk of developing hypothermia is visited regularly or taken care of.

It is heartening to note that in the winter of 1986, 400 dustmen in Birmingham, as an experiment, ensured that the elderly were safe during the cold months. A few years ago trade union leaders called on 17,000 refuse collectors in the rest of the country to follow the Birmingham example.

Once hypothermia has developed the management includes slow warming, treatment with antibiotics and the provision of adequate fluids. This is ideally done in a hospital's general ward. It is suggested that the use of intensive care beds should not be considered necessary to manage such patients except in severe cases (i.e. when core temperature is below 32°C when patients should clearly be managed as an emergency).

After successful rewarming the patient should have reassessment of his or her medical condition, because at this stage the condition causing hypothermia may become obvious and need treatment. It is prudent to avoid alcohol.

Prior to discharge from hospital, a review of the patient's *home circumstances and domiciliary support should be a 'must' to help* prevent the condition recurring.

Summary

1. Improvements of adverse social circumstances (e.g. inadequate nutrition and poor housing conditions) will go a long way to decreasing the incidence of hypothermia in the elderly.

2. We should consider the overall mortality rate due to cold weather rather than just concentrating on hypothermia. Many elderly people may not realise the potential hazards of exposure to cold outside their homes. This should be explained to them and advice regarding adequate clothing, i.e. wearing woollen hats and gloves and sensible footwear with thick socks should be emphasised.

3. The public should be educated about the adverse effects of cold weather, in the form of discussions on television and radio, over and above what is currently being done in newspapers and magazines.

4. The season of good will towards the neighbours, especially elderly people, should not just last for two weeks over Christmas. This should be spread out evenly over the whole of the winter season and preferably all the year round. It is heartening to note that the Government is committed to paying people of pensionable age towards heating their houses, (this is linked to their benefit) during winter months.

Final message

1. Physiological changes associated with ageing, presence of chronic diseases and concomitant use of several drugs make the elderly prone to hypothermia.

2. Clinical death due to 'low body temperature' is not synonymous with biological death and it is important to realise that hypothermia can mimic death in all aspects (including flat E.E.G and asystole), hence aggressive efforts should be made to resuscitate such patients - especially those acutely hypothermic.

References/Further reading list

1. 'Winter mortality: warm housing offers cold comfort', Bill Keatinge, *Geriatric Medicine*, December 1987.

2. 'Hypothermia and elderly people', Kalman, K. *Practitioner*, June 1987.

3. *The Independent*, December 22, 1987.

4. *Environmental Emergencies*. Nelson, Rund and Keller - 1985; W.B. Saunders, Philadelphia.

5. *Clinics in Geriatric Medicine* (clinical illness with elderly issue) February 1994, W.B. Saunders Co. Philadelphia.

6. Management of Profound Hypothermia (H. Antretter *et al.*) *British Journal of Hospital Medicine*, 1995; Vol. 54 (Pages 215–220)

Sexuality in the Elderly

In the past, studies and views on sex and elderly people have been myths and misunderstandings. Happily, these are changing. No doubt, there are both quantitative and qualitative changes in both sexes as one gets older. However, these changes are very individual, as with other body systems, and a qualitative sense of sexual enjoyment can be well maintained even to a very old age. The most common cause of erectile dysfunction, i.e. impotence, is vascular, including cardiovascular causes but also diabetes, prostate and bowel operations, alcohol abuse and smoking. (The prevalence of erectile dysfunction is over 50 per cent in men aged 50–70 years.)

The recent interest in the use of Viagra has been enormous – and the evidence on its effectiveness is good. This drug is currently not available on NHS prescription only to those under specified category. Any drug may have side effects and Viagra is no exception. People using it should be properly assessed, especially regarding their cardiovascular status and they should not be taking drugs like nitrates for the treatment of their angina. Long-term safety and effectiveness of the drug should be monitored by researchers.

[Source: 1. Chapter on, Sexuality in the Elderly in *A Guide to Care of the Elderly* (eds. R. B. Shukla and D. Brooks)
H.M.S.O., 1996

2. Viagra - on release
Editorial, *British Medical Journal* 19 September 1998.]

3. UK issues guidance on prescribing Viagra. *British Medical Journal*; January 30, 1999, p.279.

Further reading list

Sexual problems associated with infertility, pregnancy and ageing – ABC of Sexual Health Series. British Medical Journal 1999; 318: 587–589

The Management of Cancer in the Elderly

CHAPTER 17

Elaine Young, MRCP, FRCR, Specialist Registrar in Clinical Oncology,

Christie Hospital, Withington, Manchester, M20 4BX, UK

This detailed Chapter has been discussed under five sections and is concluded by a general summary.

Section 1: Introduction

Cancer has recently overtaken heart disease as the leading cause of death in the UK (1996 data). The death rate from both conditions is falling but at different rates. Many of these deaths are preventable, either by reducing risk factors such as smoking, or by improved standards of care.

Cancer is often thought of as a disease of middle age, and it is of course a significant cause of early death. What is not so well known is that the majority of malignancies actually arise in the elderly, with a steady increase in the age-specific incidence of most cancers. (That means that although the number of patients with cancer aged 75 might be lower than at 55, because the number of people in the UK aged 75 is lower, the likelihood of getting cancer at this age is actually higher). Seventy per cent of new cases of cancer occur in people aged over 60 years and at least 30 per cent in over 70s.

The number of old people is increasing steadily; currently 15 per cent of the UK population is over 70 years old, and the proportion of older elderly, i.e. over 85 years, is expected to have increased by 50 per cent in the 1990s. It seems unlikely that the incidence of cancer will fall dramatically in the short term, and the cost of treatment is likely to increase as newer drugs are introduced and the elderly are offered more intensive therapy.

The management of the young elderly person (under 75) with cancer is not very different to that of the younger patient, as most people in this age group can tolerate surgery and radiotherapy very well. A common misconception is that cancer in the elderly is more benign than in younger patients, but this is simply not the case, and inadequate treatment should be avoided.

The life expectancy of a 70-year-old woman is about 14 years and even at 80 a woman can expect to live for another 8 years, so many useful life years can be lost by late diagnosis or insufficient treatment. A French study suggested that 16 per cent of women over 75 with breast cancer have inappropriate management.

When considering a patient for treatment, the biological or physiological age is more important than chronological age in deciding the likely tolerance of the various therapies. Although about 50 per cent of cancer patients over 70 years have at least one other medical problem, not all of these affect the management. There is a definite reduction in renal function as we age and this affects how chemotherapy and other drugs are handled. Diabetic patients have more problems with steroids and some chemotherapy, particularly vincristine and drugs which can damage the nervous system. Several drugs have a deleterious affect on the heart so should be avoided in patients with known ischaemic heart disease.

Social circumstances also change as we age, with many people living alone with few close relations still alive. Eighty per cent of 80 year olds remain in the community although many of these will be fairly dependent on family for support and may themselves be housebound.

Personal perspectives change too and most elderly people have experienced at least one friend or relation suffering from cancer. If this was an unpleasant experience it might deter a person from seeking help for symptoms which they suspect to be due to cancer. Data certainly show that tumours are generally more advanced at time of diagnosis in the elderly. Education and improved symptom control should help.

The risk factors for cancer in the elderly are very similar to those in younger people; in particular, smoking, which accounts for 30 per cent of cancer deaths at all ages. Inherited gene abnormalities are relatively less important but elderly people have had longer exposures to common carcinogens and simply being old is the most important risk factor of all!

The first consideration when deciding all cancer treatment is "Can this patient be cured?" This can be interpreted as controlling all symptoms of the disease until death occurs of another cause. The danger in the elderly is that a patient might be expected to succumb to heart disease perhaps within a few years of diagnosis of a malignant tumour and treatment may, therefore be chosen that is not aimed at cure. This can lead to the situation where further surgery is required five years later in a patient who is now older and less fit then at first. This situation should be avoided at all costs.

Section 2: The most common conditions
Common tumour types remain common in the elderly, but the rarer cancers tend to be more age specific. For instance, teratomas are not seen past middle age and myeloma and prostate cancer are extremely rare before it.

Lung, breast, colon, stomach, pancreas and oesophagus are common primary cancer sites, and on the whole the treatment is similar to that of younger patients. A brief outline of some of these cancers is given below.

Cancers arising in the head and neck region or pelvis present more difficult management problems in the elderly as the treatment can be very toxic.

Skin tumours are very common in the elderly, being related to the duration of exposure to ultraviolet light. Melanoma is less important in this age group, but even the seemingly more benign basal and squamous cell carcinomas can be difficult to control if neglected.

The successful treatment of lymphoma is very dependent on the use of chemotherapy and a careful assessment of the patient's general condition is required before some of the more toxic agents are used. With care and support, symptomatic benefit can be achieved and maintained for some time with a combination of reduced dose chemotherapy and limited radiotherapy. Some important cancers are now discussed.

Breast cancer

The incidence of breast cancer is highest in older women, with 60 per cent of tumours being diagnosed over the age of 65 years. Currently screening stops at age 65 in the UK, but this policy might be revised in the near future as evidence mounts that compliance with the screening programme is better than expected in older women. More tumours in older patients present with negative lymph nodes, and more are low-grade, oestrogen-positive, tumours which tend to have a better prognosis. This should lead to an overall improvement in prognosis in the elderly. In practical terms this does not seem to be the case, possibly because this cancer is undertreated, but also because elderly people frequently have other medical problems.

Localised disease In general the first line treatment for a patient with localised breast cancer is surgical. The options include:
1. Mastectomy
2. Wide local excision with or without radiotherapy
3. Adding axillary surgery: clearance or sampling of the lymph nodes under the arm

In any case, the addition of tamoxifen is now routine. It is a hormone and acts on oestrogen receptors on the surface of tumour cells, blocking oestrogen and leading to death of tumour cells. It has its greatest effect in women over 50 years, and in those tumours proven to have oestrogen receptors. Tamoxifen improves survival by 10–20 per cent. It improves local control and reduces the incidence of metastatic disease. Chemotherapy on the other hand has very little benefit in the adjuvant setting, i.e. straight after surgery, in the elderly.

There is a small group of patients who, because of their frailty, advanced age, or co-existing medical conditions, are not felt to be fit for any surgical procedure. In these patients tamoxifen alone can be used. This will shrink the breast tumour in about 70 per cent of cases. However, the five-year control rate is only 30 per cent: this is obviously insufficient in a fit 70 year old who can expect to live for up to 15 years. This approach, 'neo-adjuvant' tamoxifen, can also be tried in large tumours which would require extensive surgery for which the patient is not fit or willing, for example if the patient refuses a mastectomy. Surgery can follow later if the patient's condition improves, or if the tumour shrinks sufficiently to allow breast-conserving surgery.

The role of radiotherapy in the elderly is uncertain, as in the majority of patients tamoxifen will control microscopic residual disease. There is no definite age above which radiotherapy is not offered, as biological age is as important as chronological age in determining which patients will experience more severe side effects.

Advanced or metastatic breast cancer in the elderly. Women developing recurrence of the tumour in the remaining breast tissue or in axillary lymph nodes can be assessed for further surgery, usually a mastectomy or axillary clearance. This can then be followed by hormone therapy, either with tamoxifen, if this has not already been used, or with a second-line hormone. If distant metastases occur they are most likely to be in bone or soft tissue and a response to tamoxifen is seen in 30-50 per cent if this has not previously been given. Consideration should be given to chemotherapy in the young elderly with secondaries in the liver or lung.

Second-line hormone therapies include progesterones, e.g. megestrol acetate 160 mg daily, and aromatase inhibitors, e.g. anastrazole 1 mg daily. These are equally effective, with response rates of around 25 per cent, but patients generally prefer the side effect profile of anastrazole, as it causes less weight gain than the progesterones do.

The chemotherapy regime that is used most frequently in the elderly is CMF (cyclophosphamide, methotrexate and 5-fluorouracil), either intravenously or orally. Careful monitoring of the blood count is essential.

Palliative radiotherapy for bony metastases or soft tissue masses is well tolerated, and can usually be given as an outpatient, often as a single fraction or 4- or 5-day course. Bone pain will improve in about 80 per cent after about two weeks.

Prostate cancer

Prostate cancer is a disease mainly of the elderly, with virtually no cases in men less than 50 years old, and 50 per cent of cases occurring over the age of 70. It is the third most common cancer in males, with 10,000 deaths in the UK each year. The incidence increased by 30 per cent over the period 1980 to 1990, with the largest increase being in the oldest age groups.

Although many cancers are found incidentally at TURP (transurethral resection of the prostate), up to 50 per cent have already metastasised at presentation. Screening younger men by measuring the blood level of PSA (prostate-specific antigen) will tend to pick up early tumours which may well have remained undetected until death; around a third of men over 75 years will have unsuspected tumour detected at autopsy.

The treatment of early, asymptomatic tumours has been heavily debated and new guidelines have been drawn up. For men with life expectancy over 10 years, radical surgery or radiotherapy should be offered. Neither of these options is without side effects and so for older patients, adopting a 'watch and wait' policy is advisable. Most patients will eventually progress to symptomatic disease, but with appropriate treatment, their life expectancy is still not significantly different from that of the general population.

Patients who have locally advanced disease or bone metastases can be managed with hormonal manipulation, which will reduce the size of the tumour and bring the PSA to normal in over 80 per cent of patients. Symptoms such as bladder outflow obstruction or pain will be relieved in these patients. Hormone treatment aims to reduce the level of circulating testosterone (male hormone). The two main options are surgical orchidectomy (castration) or the use of LHRH (luteinising hormone releasing hormone) antagonists such as goserelin or buserelin. Goserelin is given as a subcutaneous implant either monthly or every three months. Side effects of either option include impotence and hot flushes. The flushes sometimes respond to the addition of a progesterone. The introduction of an LHRH analogue must be covered with a short course of an anti-androgen, such as cyproterone acetate, to cover the sudden surge in testosterone and potential tumour flare which might cause acute urinary retention or spinal cord compression.

The most common site of metastatic spread is to the bones. Metastases from a prostate cancer are typically sclerotic (white on plain X-ray) and most frequently affect the spine and pelvis. The PSA is almost always elevated, often over 100 μg/l, and opiate analgesia is often required for the pain. Response to hormone manipulation is maintained for 2 years on average. Relapse is inevitable, and prognosis then is around 9 months. Radiotherapy is very useful and can be directed at a particular site of pain, or given to a large area, such as the whole pelvis, lumbar spine and upper femora, the 'lower hemibody'. A single fraction is sufficient for pain control. Radioactive strontium can be given by intravenous injection if the pain is widespread, but is only available in limited centres at present.

The response to second-line hormones is poor, and symptomatic treatment is probably as effective.

Lung cancer

Lung cancer is still the most common cause of cancer death in men over 65 years and is now the second, behind breast cancer, in women. There were 32,000 deaths from lung cancer in England in1991. Although the death rate in men is falling due to a reduction in the number of smokers, it continues to rise in women and in the over 75s.

The prognosis is dismal in all ages, with a five-year survival rate of less than 10 per cent. The best hope for long-term survival is surgery, but the elderly are unlikely to be fit for pneumonectomy (removal of a whole lung), and they are less likely than a younger person is, to be referred for a surgical opinion. Overall in the UK only 10 per cent are treated surgically.

Symptoms of lung cancer are cough, shortness of breath, chest pain, or haemoptysis (coughing up blood). Eighty per cent of cases are caused by smoking, and many of the patients are accustomed to a chronic cough, so medical attention might not be sought immediately. New symptoms lasting more than about two weeks or a bout of bronchitis that fails to settle after antibiotics should prompt further investigation.

Most lung cancers are detected on a simple chest X-ray, and confirmed with bronchoscopy: (a fibreoptic telescope inserted through the nose into the bronchial tree). This can be done as an out patient with local anaesthetic and is generally well tolerated, even by the elderly or frail. Biopsy can be done at the same time if the tumour is seen, or washings can be taken from the abnormal lung. Sputum can also be sent for cytology (microscopic examination) when malignant cells might be seen.

For the majority of patients, only palliative treatment is possible. This includes giving radiotherapy to the primary tumour or to secondaries (e.g. in bone, soft tissue, or brain), steroids and pain-killers. Radiotherapy can be given either as a single fraction or a short course, both of which are convenient and well tolerated. Effusions (fluid around the lung) are common and can be drained easily, with pleurodesis (sticking the lung surface to the rib cage) if they recur.

Radical radiotherapy is offered to patients with early stage tumours who are medically unfit for surgery, and can give results comparable to surgery, with a 20 per cent five-year survival rate.

About 25 per cent of tumours are slightly different, called small cell lung cancer (or oat cell). These are more aggressive tumours, which metastasise (spread) early and have a very poor prognosis: only 8 per cent of patients survive five years. These tumours do, however, respond to chemotherapy, and this should be considered, even in an elderly patient, as the symptomatic relief can justify the side effects of nausea, hair loss and infection risk. Oral etoposide was previously the standard palliative regime, but a recent MRC study suggests that a more intensive intravenous regime can give a better quality of life and slightly longer survival.

The government has set targets for the reduction in smoking and in the death rate from lung cancer in the under 75 age group by the year 2010. In practice, however, it is likely to be a lot longer before we see a dramatic reduction in the disease in the elderly.

Colon cancer

This is another tumour that starts to appear in middle age but which increases in incidence steadily with age. If detected early, with the tumour still confined within the bowel wall, (i.e. Duke's stage A), the prognosis is excellent. Unfortunately, currently about 80 per cent of tumours are not identified until they have spread to the lymph nodes, (which is Duke's stage C), or to the liver. The survival in stage C tumours is less than 40 per cent at 5 years. The average survival of a patient with liver metastases is 6 to 9 months without treatment.

The symptoms of bowel cancer are change in bowel habit, abdominal discomfort and rectal bleeding. Diagnosis is usually made with colonoscopy and biopsy or by seeing the typical appearance on a barium enema X-ray.

Treatment is primarily surgical with a bowel resection, with or without colostomy, which can sometimes be reversed. A few elderly patients are not fit for radical surgery; but in general, it is safer to do a planned resection than to leave a tumour *in situ* which might go on to cause obstruction, requiring emergency surgery on an ill patient.

In younger patients, the role for chemotherapy is now becoming clear, with adjuvant chemotherapy with 5-fluorouracil and folinic acid being offered to all patients with lymph node involvement, in a similar way to patients with breast cancer. Patients in their 70s who are otherwise fit seem to tolerate the side effects – diarrhoea and a sore mouth and eyes – surprisingly well. Treatment is usually given weekly as an outpatient for 6 months.

Likewise, palliative chemotherapy is offered to the majority of younger patients when they develop liver metastases. The doses required in this case are higher and the benefits less clear-cut. Because of this, in the elderly, treatment is often deferred if the metastases are not causing symptoms. An increase in life expectancy, from 6 months to around a year, is all that can realistically be expected, and if there is significant pain or nausea, these can be usefully treated.

Section 3: Various ways of treating cancer

Radiotherapy

This is the use of ionising radiation to kill tumour cells. Early treatments were with natural sources of radioactivity such as radium. Nowadays most treatment is given using X-rays produced at very high energy levels by machines known as linear accelerators. These machines produce a focused X-ray beam, which penetrates tissue causing damage to the genetic content of cells and causing them to die. By splitting the total dose of irradiation into many small fractions, which are most commonly given once a day, the normal tissues surrounding the tumour are spared and recover.

Most courses of treatment are spread over 2 to 6 weeks, although single fractions entailing just one visit to the radiotherapy department are very useful in palliating symptoms of advanced or metastatic cancer. It is often the prolonged nature of the treatment that is a problem for the elderly patient who might not have ready access to transport, especially if the distance involved is great. The main advantage of the longest courses of therapy is the reduction in the late side effects. These may be less important in many elderly patients, as the life expectancy is less. Besides, elderly people tend to be less concerned with the cosmetic result.

Side effects are predictable and usually controllable with simple medication. Any treatment to the throat or mediastinum (the centre of the chest) will cause inflammation of the oesophagus and pain on swallowing. Similarly radiotherapy to the abdomen or pelvis will affect the bowel and give rise to diarrhoea. Treatment given to the skin will result in redness and weeping, and treatment to the scalp will result in hair loss. However, in general, all the acute side effects start during the second or third week of treatment and settle 4 to 6 weeks after completion.

Chemotherapy

This term only really means the use of drugs to kill cells and used to include antibiotic therapy too. It has come to be associated with nasty drugs given by a drip which cause a great deal of sickness, hair loss and is worse than the cancer it is trying to cure. In some conditions, notably testicular tumours and leukaemias, the expectation of cure is high and such toxic treatments are used, (but the control of the side effects is now excellent). The majority of cancers can be treated with less toxic regimes which can be successfully modified to suit the elderly patient.

In the last decade the introduction of newer anti-sickness drugs, such as ondansetron and granisetron, which are serotonin (5-HT$_3$) antagonists, has revolutionised the use of chemotherapy and we can assure patients that they will have minimal chemotherapy-induced vomiting. Drugs have been developed, and are in routine use, which can boost the production of white blood cells and help greatly to reduce the number of septic episodes in more intensive regimes (even hair loss can be prevented by the use of scalp cooling during the administration of chemotherapy.) Most chemotherapy is now given by specially trained nurses.

Almost all chemotherapy regimes cause myelosuppression – temporary damage to the bone marrow. This results in increased susceptibility to infection and all patients are warned of this and should seek urgent medical attention at the first sign of fever. The treatment is empirical intravenous administration of broad-spectrum antibiotics, commonly imipenem or a combination of an aminoglycoside with piperacillin. The effect on red blood cells and platelets is less dramatic, occurs later in the course of treatment, and can be treated with transfusion of blood or platelets as appropriate.

Several drugs are toxic to the heart, including 5-fluorouracil (5-FU), which is standard treatment for metastatic bowel cancer, and doxorubicin, which is very effective in non-Hodgkin's lymphoma and breast cancer. If there is a previous history of coronary artery disease these agents should be avoided. Doxorubicin and a similar drug, epirubicin, are very toxic in jaundiced patients, but liver metastases without obstruction are not a contraindication. Methotrexate is a standard first-line drug in breast cancer and is also useful in squamous cell cancers of any origin, but is excreted into effusions and slowly released back into the blood stream. This so-called third space effect increases its toxicity and must be considered. Cisplatin and vincristine both cause peripheral nerve damage and this is much worse in diabetic patients.

One tumour where chemotherapy in the elderly is now well tolerated is ovarian cancer. Standard therapy was cisplatin, which is toxic to kidneys and nerves and requires to be given with a large volume of fluid. Now carboplatin has been found to be equally effective, is much better tolerated, can be given on an outpatient basis, and the dose is calculated according to the renal function, not the weight, of the patient, so any deterioration with age is automatically allowed for.

Surgery
The main treatment for most cancers remains surgery. Most elderly patients will tolerate appropriate radical surgery given adequate pre-operative assessment and stabilisation of other medical problems, such as hypertension and diabetes. If a patient is deemed unfit for, say, mastectomy and axillary node clearance, then a simple mastectomy or lumpectomy followed by radiotherapy and hormone treatment will suffice. Likewise, local excision of a rectal tumour can provide symptomatic benefit while being much less traumatic than an abdomino-pelvic resection and colostomy. Many procedures can be done under local or spinal anaesthetic, avoiding the need for a general anaesthetic, although modern techniques mean that, if necessary, almost any elderly person can be anaesthetised safely.

Section 4: Palliative care

Pain control
Not all patients with cancer have pain but it is one of the most feared aspects of the disease. However, it can usually be readily controlled. The most important part of pain management in cancer patients is careful assessment. The site, nature and probable cause of the pain all affect the type of analgesic (pain-killer) that is most likely to be effective.

Bone pain, soft tissue pain and nerve pain can be differentiated and managed in parallel.

One of the most useful concepts in palliative care is:

"By the clock, by mouth and by the ladder".

This implies that pain-relieving drugs should be given regularly, before the patient is able to experience pain. This sounds impossible but once pain control is stabilised, it is actually fairly easy to achieve. Secondly, always try to avoid giving drugs by injection, which only adds to the patient's distress. The ladder referred to is the WHO (World Health Organisation) pain ladder, which suggests a way to increase the strength of analgesics until the correct level has been reached:

1. Simple analgesics, e.g. paracetamol, to start with.

2. Add weak opioids, e.g. codeine phosphate in moderate dosage.

3. Change to strong opioids, e.g. morphine or fentanyl.

Plus: Adjuvant use of co-analgesics, e.g. non-steroidal anti-inflammatory drugs, antidepressants.

Some types of pain are not opiate-responsive. The most difficult pain to control is probably that of infiltration of nerves themselves by tumour, for example recurrent breast cancer in the brachial plexus (the bundle of nerves under the arm). Referral to a specialist in pain control, or a consultant in palliative care, is always advised. The hospice movement and Macmillan nurse services have developed particular expertise in pain control and should usually be involved.

Morphine is the mainstay of pain control in advanced cancer. There is no upper dose limit, and neither tolerance nor addiction seems to be a problem in patients with severe pain. Morphine is available in two types of oral preparation: rapid acting or slow release. Morphine sulphate solution is the usual starting point. It gives pain relief within 20 minutes and is effective for about four hours. The dose can be increased as required, aiming at complete freedom from pain. The dose required in a day is then converted to slow release morphine with the solution then being used for so-called breakthrough pain. Most patients experience some nausea and drowsiness when first starting opiates, but this quickly wears off. Whenever opiates are used, attention must be paid to the bowels (as morphine causes constipation) and a laxative such as co-danthramer should be prescribed from the start.

For pain arising from bones or soft tissue, non-steroidal anti-inflammatory drugs can be added. Ibuprofen, naproxen and diclofenac are the most commonly used. Care must be taken as many patients are also taking steroids and there is then an increased risk of peptic ulceration and/or dyspeptic symptoms.

For nerve pain a variety of drugs have been tried, such as amitriptyline and carbamazepine. Specialist techniques such as nerve blocks or spinal anaesthesia can help in the most difficult cases.

The development of the subcutaneous infusion given using a syringe driver has proved extremely useful in patients who are unable to take drugs orally. Diamorphine is used for pain as it is more soluble, and the dose of oral morphine can be converted using a simple formula. Other agents, such as anti-sickness drugs and sedatives, can also be administered by this route.

Palliative radiotherapy is most effective against pain from bone metastases and any treatment with an effect on the tumour, such as hormone therapy or palliative chemotherapy will give some reduction in pain.

Cough and shortness of breath

These symptoms can be very distressing to the cancer patient, and occur in 80 per cent of patients with lung cancer and in up to 50 per cent of all patients with advanced cancer. Many tumour types give rise to secondaries in the lungs, or to pleural effusions (fluid around the lung), or to disease in the lymph system within the chest.

Cough can be due to mechanical irritation of the linings of the lungs at any point, to infection, or to complications of treatment such as radiation fibrosis. Treatment is aimed at relieving the symptom and this does not always mean treating the tumour itself. Physiotherapy and postural drainage can help to clear secretions. The viscosity of the mucus can be reduced with nebulised saline or other mucolytics. Cough suppressants, such as opiates or inhaled bupivacaine (a local anaesthetic), will relieve a distressing symptom, which can be especially severe at night.

Shortness of breath has many causes, such as obstruction of the airways, reduction in lung volume by effusions, reduced ability of the lung tissue to absorb oxygen (e.g. because of lymphangitis) or a sensation of difficulty in breathing can be caused by anxiety or panic attacks. The first part of treatment is to ensure the patient has a relaxed environment and feels secure and safe. Treatable causes should be dealt with appropriately, e.g. infections and effusions. Morphine, steroids, anxiolytics such as diazepam and oxygen can all be useful in reducing the sensation of breathlessness.

Nausea, vomiting and anorexia
Sixty per cent of patients with advanced cancer experience nausea and vomiting at some time, either due to the disease or the drugs used to treat it. Understanding the cause of the sickness helps to identify the appropriate management. Bowel obstruction is sometimes caused by tumour in the abdomen or within the bowel, but can also be caused by severe constipation. Hypercalcaemia, renal failure, opiate analgesics, chemotherapy and raised intracranial pressure (due to brain tumours) all result in nausea.

Once mechanical problems have been dealt with as fully as possible, bearing in mind that surgery for bowel obstruction is not always advisable, there are many different types of antiemetics to choose from. The drugs act on a variety of receptors at different sites within the central nervous system or in the gastro-intestinal tract. Metoclopramide increases gastric emptying, cyclizine is very useful in obstruction, haloperidol (at low doses, 1.5 – 3 mg) is most useful in nausea due to morphine, and methotrimeprazine is an excellent anti-emetic but causes sedation in half the patients. Many agents can be given by subcutaneous infusion and domperidone is available as a suppository.

Anorexia in advanced cancer can lead to cachexia although this has other causes not directly related to the calorific intake of the patient. Small portions, well presented, can be supplemented with high calorie drinks. Steroids and progesterones, such as megestrol acetate, can improve the appetite and lead to weight gain. In the terminal stages of cancer it is important to stress to the carers that there is little to be gained from forcing a patient to eat against his will, and it is more important to ensure good mouth care with mouthwashes and anti-fungal agents for the patient's comfort.

Difficulty in swallowing can be helped, if it is due to obstruction of the oesophagus by tumour, with stenting, laser therapy, dilatation and radiotherapy. Even with these measures a liquidised diet might still be necessary.

Oncological emergencies
Various emergencies can occur in the course of cancer treatment. Important among these are:
1. *Spinal cord compression* Although this is a rare complication of cancer it is devastating and can only be reversed if treated early in the onset of symptoms. Tumour in the spine, either in the bones or a soft tissue mass, compresses the spinal cord and results in loss of power and sensation in the legs, combined with loss of function of the bowel and bladder. The first symptoms are sensory and then progressive weakness of the legs follows. The most accurate imaging technique is magnetic resonance scanning, which clearly delineates the level of compression. Urgent treatment should be started

with high dose steroids (dexamethasone 16 mg daily) followed by referral for radiotherapy which is most likely to be effective if given within 24 – 48 hours of the onset of symptoms. Catheterisation is usually necessary and the prognosis is generally very poor.

2. *Superior vena cava obstruction* This is obstruction of the flow of blood draining the upper body to the heart and is caused either by compression of the vena cava (the main vein in the chest) or by thrombus (blood clot) within it. The symptoms are swelling of the head and neck, dilated veins across the chest and headaches. Steroids should be started immediately and in patients with a known primary tumour, radiotherapy can be given urgently. Radiological stenting of the vena cava is extremely effective in relieving the symptoms and can be used in combination with or instead of radiotherapy. If thrombus is found, anticoagulation is advised but the results are not as good.

3. *Hypercalcaemia* A raised level of calcium in the blood can occur in many cancers, especially if bony secondaries are present. The symptoms are nausea and vomiting, drowsiness and confusion. It is seen most commonly in patients with breast cancer and can be effectively treated with hydration and intravenous bisphosphonates, e.g. pamidronate. Once normal, it can be maintained by actively treating the cancer, e.g. with hormone therapy in breast or prostate cancer, or by continuing with oral bisphosphonates such as clodronate. Ensuring adequate fluid intake is very important and can help to prevent recurrence of symptomatic hypercalcaemia.

4. *Pathological fracture* Whenever tumour deposits are identified in the long bones of the arm or leg, attention must be paid to the degree of cortical thinning (destruction of the weight-bearing part of the bone). If the cortex is significantly destroyed thought should be given to prophylactic radiotherapy or to orthopaedic intervention with pinning of the bone. Such bones, especially the femur

and humerus can fracture spontaneously without a significant fall, and would then require emergency surgery. This can be devastating, more so in the elderly as they would then have a greater risk from general anaesthesia.

Section 5: Government initiatives

Screening

It might seem surprising to discuss screening in a book about the elderly, as up to now this has been something offered to younger people. It is said that the main reason not to offer breast screening with mammography to women over 65 years is because of the low compliance rate. This may not be the case, as several studies have now found take-up rates of 70 per cent among older women, and with the increased prevalence of breast cancer in older women the benefits are likely to be at least as high. The number of life years saved by the early detection of a breast cancer in an elderly woman, who might well be destined to die within 5 years of a coronary thrombosis, is undoubtedly less than for a fit 50-year-old woman. But extending the upper age limit for screening will probably be more cost-effective than starting the screening programme at 40.

Other diseases where screening is possible include prostate and colon cancer. An elevated PSA in an elderly man might prompt a search for the diagnosis of an early prostate cancer, only to find that a watch and wait policy is then adopted. But in younger men with a life expectancy of over ten years it seems likely that some sort of national screening programme will be in place in the near future.

Screening for colon cancer, by a simple test for blood in the stools, is probably one of the most cost-effective methods of reducing mortality. However, the patient should be aware that the next step: colonoscopy and biopsy, is not without risk, and especially so in the more elderly population. It is estimated that national screening would change the balance of stages at diagnosis from the majority being Duke's C to an even split across the stages, and this would obviously improve the survival rates. A pilot study of faecal occult blood testing is about to be introduced in selected regions.

Health of the nation initiatives
Several cancers were singled out for discussion in the Government's White Paper and objectives for improved care and prevention were established. However, the main thrust was aimed at people under the age of 60 years. For instance in breast cancer the target was a 25 per cent reduction in mortality, but only in "women invited for screening". As the upper age limit for invitation to screening is 64 years this effectively excludes elderly women completely.

Lung cancers were also included but mainly from a preventive approach by reducing the proportion of the population that smokes.

The aim with skin cancer was to halt the year on year increase in incidence and mortality, aimed at both melanoma and non-melanoma cancers.

To make any real impact on the survival of elderly patients with cancer it is vital that awareness of the most appropriate treatment is increased among doctors and patients alike. This does not seem to be the case, possibly because that cancer is undertreated, but also because elderly people frequently have other medical problems.

Calman–Hine Report
In 1995 the Government commissioned a report by the expert advisory group on cancer which gives guidance on the future structure of cancer services in the UK. The aim is to create a network of care in England and Wales which will ensure that all patients, regardless of where they live, will receive care of a uniformly high standard.

This policy framework proposes that Cancer Units within district general hospitals will treat common cancers, and patients with less common tumours will be referred to one of 30 Cancer Centres for specialist care. The centres will serve a population of approximately one million, and radiotherapy services will be centralised here. It has been established that implementing these reforms will require additional funding in the region of £200 million.

Summary

1. The older we get, the more likely we are to suffer from cancer. About one in three people in the UK will develop cancer in their lifetime and one in four will die from it.

2. If you are worried that you or a relative has cancer, then you must get help early. Many suspected cancers are actually benign lesions which are not life threatening. Only proper investigation can confirm this. If cancer is found, then the outlook is always better if it is found before it has spread.

3. Older people should not be excluded from a screening programme of proven value, or denied effective treatment once the diagnosis of cancer has been made. To make any real impact on the survival of elderly patients with cancer it is vital that awareness of the most appropriate treatment is increased among doctors and patients alike.

4. Cancer reform is lagging behind in this country despite the Calman Report's recommendations. All patients, including the elderly, should have access to high quality management of their cancer in a specialist unit. The Government must provide the extra funding required.

5. Considerable advances have been made in the detection and treatment of cancer in recent years. The use of chemotherapy in the early stages of breast cancer, for example, can reduce the recurrence rate and mortality of women. The benefit is not just limited to young patients. The employment of Cancer Specialist Nurses has been an immense help in improving patient information, palliative care and the delivery of chemotherapy. The

hospice movement is well developed in the UK and is not only for the dying patient.

6. Prevention can be primary, i.e. lifestyle changes to prevent the development of cancer, or secondary, i.e. detecting potential cancers at an early stage. The first is difficult in practice in the elderly (dietary changes, exercise) or impossible (even ex-smokers have an increased risk of lung cancer). But early detection can be achieved in many cases.

7. Management of cancer at every stage requires close liaison between many different health professionals: physicians, surgeons and pathologists at the time of diagnosis, cancer specialists for chemo- and radiotherapy, and support from psychologists and palliative care teams. The integration of all these teams and excellent communication with the general practitioner/family doctor will improve the standard of care received by the patient.

8. Finally, the aim of treatment is not only to increase the duration of life of the elderly patient with cancer; the quality of the final years is equally, if not more, important. There is no consensus yet on this topic as it means different things to different people. The patient must have the last word: in his/her judgement are the side effects of treatment worth the benefits? Research continues into this difficult subject.

Final message
1. Many cancers can be prevented.
2. Do not ignore symptoms in the elderly.
3. Early expert help and advice should be sought and this should be available.
4. Look for treatable tumours – elderly patients can tolerate fairly radical surgery.
5. Even the elderly will go through a lot for a chance of increasing their life span.
6. Radiotherapy is effective and can be modified for the elderly.
7. Give adequate analgesia, regularly.
8. Understanding the biology of cancer will help to use treatments in future instead of currently used (i.e. empirically derived) cancer-killing drugs and radiation therapies.

Useful addresses

1. BACUP (British Association of Cancer United Patients)

3 Bath Place, Rivington Street,
London EC2A 3JR
BACUP Website: www.cancerbacup.org.uk
(Freephone Cancer Information Service:
0800 18 11 99)

2. Cancerlink

11–21 Northdown Street,
London N1 9BN
Tel Freephone Cancer Information Helpline:
0800 132905
Tel Asian Cancer Information Helpline:
0800 590415

3. Macmillan Cancer Relief

Anchor House,
15/19 Britten Street,
London SW3 3TZ
Tel 0171 351 7811

References/Further reading list

1. *Oxford Textbook of Oncology*, Chapter 8, Cancer in the Elderly (Ed. Michael Peckham), 1995 ISBN 0-19-236 1685-4 (O.U.P.)

2. *Oxford Textbook of Palliative Medicine* (Ed. Derek Doyle *et al.*) (2nd edition) ISBN 0-19-26 2566-7 (O.U.P.)

3. *Cancer in the Elderly*, Caird F.I. and Brewin T.B., Butterworth 1990 ISBN 0-7236-0972-1

4. Investigation and treatment of cancer in old age by Margot Gosney, Editorial in *Age and Ageing* 1998: 27: 417–419

5. Cancer Reforms Lag Behind – a feature article in *Hospital Medicine* (17th September, 1998 issue) by Professor Karol Sikora.

6. Twycross, R. & Lack S. (1990) *Therapeutics in Terminal Cancer* 2nd edition. Churchill Livingstone.

7. Twycross, R. (1997) *Symptom Management in Advanced Cancer* 2nd edition. Radcliffe Medical Press.

8. *Guidelines for Managing Cancer Pain in Adults.* Working Party on Clinical Guidelines in Palliative Care. 2nd edition (1998). National Council for Hospice and Specialist Palliative Care Services. (N.C.H.S.P.C.S.)

9. Kaye (P) (1994) *A to Z of Hospice and Palliative Medicine* 2nd edition. ELP Publications.

10. Prostate Screening for all? Editorial, *Update for General Practitioners*, 9th September 1998 issue, 244.

11. *Lancet* 19th Sept. 1998 issue.

12. Calman–Hine Report A Policy Framework for Commissioning Cancer Services from the Chief Medical Officer's Expert Advisory Group on Cancer in 1995.

13. Oncology – recent advances (by H. N. Martin Tattersall and H. Thomas in *Br Med J*, 13th Feb. 1999 issue.

Useful booklet

The Cancer Guide – Information for people with cancer and those who care, by Simon Crompton; B.B.C. Educational Developments, 1997.

About Terminally Ill Patient

"Giving effective pain and symptom control is very satisfying. It is rewarding to see an anxious and dying patient come to terms with his or her illness and share this with the family. The dying have much to teach us about the meaning of life, for it is at this time that people are at their more mature and their most courageous".

[Source: Symptom Management and Palliative Care by Mary J. Bairnes in *Oxford Textbook of Geriatric Medicine* (Eds. J. Grimley Evans and T. Franklin Williams). OUP, 1992.]

Communication

Not long ago, it was rightly suggested in a British Telecom advertisement that the ability to talk is a gift that no other creature on this planet shares. Providing the right message, is an important ingredient in any business. In this chapter, communication has been discussed in its broadest possible sense: apart from improving our communication skills with patients we should take advantage of the current developments in information technologies like the Internet, Tele-medicine, Tele-monitoring and many others. All these will ultimately lead to not only improved patient-care but also be cost-effective. These days we come across the following phrases almost daily: medical audit, team briefing, resource management initiative, mentoring, leadership, cost-effectiveness, managed-care, good communication and lately, clinical governance. Undoubtedly, these phrases have since assumed increasing importance for efficient running of the N.H.S.

Of these, communication is an important ingredient of effective health care and for obvious reasons, nowhere is communication more important than in the care of an older patient, e.g. in history-taking, discussing diagnosis, drug therapy and so on. Besides, as doctors are also required to give talks, teach junior colleagues, give at times evidence in Court and may occasionally need to talk to journalists, effective communication seems to form part and parcel of our working life. At any rate, there is no denying the fact that speaking or writing with precision can bring desired dividends.

Problems defined

In this chapter I have highlighted the importance of effective communication, both verbal and written. It is discussed under the following headings:

1. Communication problems in patients themselves due to effect of diseases, disability, or even ageing itself.

2. Communication problems between the various members of the health-care team (especially among the doctors) and the patients.

3. The role of managers/administrators.

All these factors are clearly interdependent and where there is a problem at one point, others are affected as well, like a fused electrical circuit.

Communication problems in the patient

There are many conditions where a patient may find difficulty in communicating with others, including:

1. *Stroke* The problem is not seen in all patients with stroke. It is seen only when there are associated sensory (perceptual) problems, motor difficulty or both. In speech problems due to sensory deficit, the patient does not understand what is being discussed or communicated. The chance for recovery in this situation is not very great and a good deal of perseverance is needed from the speech therapist, and indeed from the relatives.

Speech problems due to motor difficulty in a stroke patient, however, can be easily manipulated by sign language; besides, this problem may improve gradually. Unfortunately, if both motor and sensory speech problems are present in a patient, this makes the communication all the more difficult.

2. *Dementia* Alzheimer's dementia is the most common type of dementia. The patient's communication with others is affected depending on the degree of dementia. In advanced cases, activities of daily living are severely affected and this greatly affects the relatives and carers.

3. *Depression* Depression may be an early feature of dementia or it may start as such.

Whilst successful treatment of depression is seen in practice, the drug treatment of depression has not matched the treatment of other psychiatric conditions such as schizophrenia. It is too early to be enthusiastic about the newer anti-depressants, including the 5-HT uptake-inhibitor type, such as Prozac (fluoxetine) in severe depression.

4. *Deafness* One of the commonest causes of deafness in the elderly is wax in the ears. Doctors should never give an audiologist a chance to write back to them that the cause of the patient's deafness is wax. This should have been discovered in the first place by the referring doctor.

Mention may be made at this stage about two daily aids which may enhance communication. These are functioning hearing aids, and regularly tested, well-fitted and clean glasses. (1)

Communication problems in relation to the health-care team

This is the central theme of this chapter.

Listening to the patients is the first requisite of effective communication between a doctor and the patient. A good deal of patience on the part of the doctor is necessary as the patient, in view of disease, disability, or even advanced age, may not be forthright in communication. Learning communication skills, therefore, is vital.

Junior hospital doctors, who will eventually pursue a career, either in hospital medicine or in general practice, should be taught communication skills. This may have been imparted to them earlier, (i.e. at a stage when they are medical students) probably by a solitary lecture which is clearly not enough. They should be taught these skills while discussing the diagnosis with patients (with cancer or other serious medical conditions) or while asking permission from relatives for a post-mortem.

Whatever may be the situation, patients or their relatives should be advised precisely and in simple terms (without using confusing jargon). Unnecessary details should be avoided. While discussing problems and specially about drugs, the advice may have to be repeated.

Diseases may need explaining on a piece of paper diagrammatically. This 'reinforcement' is essential because patients are usually anxious and it is quite difficult for them to take in all the information, especially if it is complicated. (Please see appendix.)

A word about patients' complaints. Most of these complaints, no doubt, stem from inadequate information given to the patients (and or relatives) about their management. These complaints are, therefore, made in an effort to know facts and also to see/ensure that similar incidents do not recur. If a complaint has already been made, one should explain the facts and if necessary apologise. An apology should not be considered as acceptance of guilt – it is simply a reflection of good manners.

What else needs to be done to improve communication?(2)
1. Patients should be supplied with information leaflets about important medical problems, such as constipation, urinary incontinence, hiatus hernia, obesity, arthritis, osteoporosis, stroke and myocardial infarction. Indeed, studies show that patients ask for and benefit from such measures.(3) Videos for patients of all ages, outlining the main points of common medical conditions are available. (6)
2. Discharge summaries – after a patient's discharge, a letter should be sent to the GP as soon as it is reasonably practicable and should contain the diagnosis, admission and discharge dates, relevant investigations, list of medications, details (if necessary) of activities of daily living, follow up or not and the Consultant's name. The last information is important in that elderly patients usually have multiple pathology and hence may need readmission sooner, when GPs may need to contact the Consultant directly.
3. Referral letters – GPs' referral letters should, apart from information on patient's symptoms, also contain important past medical history, (including recent hospital attendance), and list of medications.
4. To avoid duplication of services to the patients the various members of the health-care team should know precisely about the needs of the patient.

5. Writing occasionally in local papers about important medical conditions goes a long way to help patients.

I cannot help mentioning an occasion when an elderly patient in the West Midlands showed me with great joy an article written by a local Geriatrician. (I had been to see her as her GP.) Clearly she had liked and appreciated the article.

Role of managers/administrators
One should not underestimate the role of managers regarding their contribution in effective communication, for the efficient running of the various services.

The managerial role may be summarised as follows:
1. Proper signposting to help patients and their relatives, both inside and outside the wards and indeed at various strategic locations in the hospital premises.
2. Provision of information leaflets about the ward and hospital, incorporating available facilities and including visiting time.
3. Information to outpatients regarding some investigative procedures, i.e. barium studies, scans etc.
4. Team briefing about patient care from time to time.
5. Some knowledge of patient's medical conditions by managers (one should not forget that managers now include doctors and other health professionals too) is necessary to advise doctors in medico-legal matters but more importantly when considering provision of services. Courses like 'Medicine for Managers' are now available and are organised both locally and nationally.
6. It is vital that liaison and consultation with medical staff are regularly maintained to avoid unnecessary misunderstanding.

Special communication (language) problems.

In many parts of the country some patients of ethnic origin, for example Asians, cannot understand the advice and information given to them because many of them neither speak nor read English.

They may be helped by specially trained interpreters and provision of written information or video in their own language will be invaluable for such patients, as would (4) sign posting in hospitals (wards, theatres etc) in ethnic languages.

Recent advances

1. *Internet* Ten million people (of all ages) in this country at present have access to the internet. The main benefit of Internet access is, of course, e-mail facility. A professional can compare notes about work/business with colleagues, both in this country and overseas. A doctor can be in touch with Academic Departments for advice and research. Keeping in mind the possibility of a strike by computer virus, one should make provision for antivirus software. Useful tips concerning the Internet are included in an article ("Tips in maximising the Internet", in Update (The Journal of Continuing Education for General Practitioners; September 9, 1998 issue; Page 290).

2. *Telecare and Telemedicine* This may be used to advise:

a. patients at home, in some cases as an alternative to attendance at outpatients

b. acute care including Telepathology. In the diagnosis of breast cancer Telepathology is a better way of having a second opinion and surer way of correct diagnosis. Here the Specialist Pathologist neither has to travel from place to place to work nor send the slide by post for interpretation/opinion. The pathologist can discuss diagnosis with another colleague who is looking at an identical slide in the patient's hospital. Not only this, while the patient is still on the operating table a surgeon can electronically send the biopsy of a cancer material for diagnosis. The cost – £50,000 for the system for each hospital. Advantage – cost effective and saving patient's lives and Consultant's time. (8)

c. Long-term care situations.

3. *Telementoring* – Surgeons can now learn from other professionals thousands of miles away. "Telementoring has the potential of demonstrating innovative techniques in a non-intrusive, interactive way, which may ultimately improve the delivery of health care as it is cost effective, brings expertise to areas where it is lacking and most importantly, speeds up health-care delivery." (7)

One hopes that the millenium bug threat to the working of NHS and other Services is sorted out soon.

Summary points

1. Good communication is thus an important ingredient of effective health care of our patients. We need better communication to improve patient care.

Happily, increasing interest is now being shown in promoting the value of communication and communication skills via meetings, symposia etc.

2. Every doctor should remember the advice given by the American psychiatrist Adolf Meyer, "when the patient and physician agree on the nature of the problem the patient gets better".

3. Adequate communication with the patient is thus the prerequisite for overall patient care. (5)

4. We should take advantage of newer information technologies.

Final message

1. Medicine, as late Professor Charles M. Fletcher said, should be seen not as a secret garden but as a subject for general debate which, as we now know, is quite true.

2. "Medicine is a science, but its practice is an art..." (Prof. Peter H. Millard). This fact needs to be kept in mind while dealing with patients and relatives.

Appendix

Improving communication with patients/relatives.

1. To start with, set the scene – ask how much they know about the patient's medical condition.

2. Explain the condition diagrammatically, avoid jargon ('Big heart' is preferable to biventricular hypertrophy).

3. Listen – conversation is always a two-way partnership.

4. Do not give unwanted advice, blame anyone, or lecture.

5. Mention all help that could be given to the patient – attendance at outpatient clinic, day hospital, or visit at home by a Specialist Nurse, if indicated (e.g. Diabetic nurse, Parkinson's disease nurse specialist or a Macmillan nurse).

6. Summarise your conversation.

7. "Do you want to ask any questions?" in the end, is very reassuring.

References

1. 'Disorders of communication in the elderly', E. Davis and J. Powell, in *Principles and Practice of Geriatric Medicine* (ed. M.S. J. Pathy. John Wiley and Sons, 1991, pp 883–93.

2. 'Lessons to learn from patient complaints', *BMA News Review*, May 1994, :25.

3. Gibbs, S., Waters, S. and George C.F., 'Communicating information to patients about medicine', *Journal of Royal Society of Medicine*, 1990, 83: 292–7.

4. Stevens, K.A. and Fletcher, R.E., 'Communicating with Asian patients', *British Medical Journal*, October 7, 1989, 299: 905–6.

5. O'Donnell, M., *Sunday Times*, October 15 1989.

6. *What you really need to know about* – Video for Patients – presented by Dr Robert Buckman (Introduced by John Cleese), available from Video for Patients Ltd., 122 Holland Park Avenue, London, W11 4VA. Tel: 0171 938 4910; Fax 0171 938 1490.

7. *Hospital Doctor*, July 9 1998

8. *The Times*, August 24 1998.

Further reading list

1. *Relating to Relatives* (Thurstan Brewin with Margaret Sparshott), Radcliffe Medical Press 1996.

2. *Communication Skills Training for Health Professionals* (D.A. Dickson, O. Hargie and N.C. Morrow). Chapman and Hall, 1989.

3. *How to do it?* Vol. 2, Third Edition. (Examination, Academia Research and Communication). B.M.J. Publishing Group, 1995

4. *The Lost Art of Healing* by Bernard Lown - Houghton Mifflin ISBN 0395 825253.

5. *Standards of Medical Care for Older People* (a booklet) Expectations and Recommendations. Published by The British Geriatric Society, February 1997.

6. *Maintaining Good Medical Practice*, General Medical Council, July, 1998.

7. *Improving Clinical Communications*. Clinical Systems Group, Department of Health N.H.S. Executive. Leeds: Department of Health, 1998.

8. *The Ulser Illusion* by Tor Norretranders - Penguin Books.

9. *Communication Skills in Medicine*. Ed. Charles R. K. Hind; B.M.J. Publishing Group, London. 176 PP £14.95.

10. *Counselling in Primary Health Care* (Ed. J. Keithley, G Marsh) Oxford University Press 1995 ISBN 019 2623540.

11. *The New Doctor – General Medical Council: Protecting Patients, Guiding Doctors;* 178 Great Portland Street, London W1N 6JE.

12. *Medicine and the Internet* - Bruce McKenzie - second edition, Price £16.95, 352 Pages (paperback) (Email to salesteam@bottinbooks.demon.co.uk.)

Rational Presribing of Drugs

CHAPTER 19

Rational prescribing is sensible and reasonable prescribing of drugs. There is no denying the fact that drugs — from humble aspirin to mighty pain-killers, antibiotics, anaesthetics, thrombolytics (blood-clot dissolving drugs), anti-AIDS drugs, interferons and many others — have helped millions from their pain, discomfort and misery. The threat to life is now much more reduced. However, it is not all plain sailing. Drugs are like double-edged swords. Every drug has a potential to give rise to adverse drug reactions or side effects. These vary from minor inconvenience to serious allergic and anaphylatic reactions which could well prove fatal.

The current National Health Service's yearly drug bill amounts to approximately £4.5 billion. We are now practising in an era of cost-containment and rightly so. Clearly this puts a tremendous responsibility on all presribing doctors. In this article I have taken a broader view on prescribing. No doubt prescribing of a drug is a challenge.

So why is prescription of a drug a challenge?

Three factors interact before a drug is prescribed for a patient:
1. *Doctor* (correct diagnosis is vitally important),
2. *Patient* (history of past medical illness, drugs taken, history of any drug allergy, e.g. penicillin),
3. *Drug itself* (several drugs are available for most of the medical conditions and a safe and effective drug has to be selected and prescribed.

Increasingly, patients are becoming more informed about the diseases and medications (and there is nothing wrong with that, I hasten to add) via magazines and books, television, radio and now the Internet (it is now becoming a popular means of finding information using personal computers, and soon one will be able to access it from the television at home). Furthermore, new drugs are being marketed, including expensive drugs for diseases like Alzheimer's dementia. New drugs are bound to be discovered and marketed, as William Withering, discoverer of digitalis, observed in 1785:

"The ingenuity of man has ever been fond of exerting itself to varied forms and combinations of medicine".

Now let us consider the various factors which a doctor must consider before a drug is prescribed. The following list is by no means comprehensive.

1. Full assessment of the patient and the correct diagnosis of the patient's problems

Correct diagnosis is the most important factor of rational prescribing. History of previous medical illnesses and drugs prescribed is very useful for current prescribing. For example, history of allergy to penicillin will be vitally important, history of asthma should be elicited if a drug such as a beta-blocker is likely to be prescribed. (Beta-blockers should not be prescribed in patients suffering from asthma.)

A history of dyspepsia will lead to caution in prescribing drugs like aspirin, anticoagulants like Warfarin and pain-killers of the anti-inflammatory group; avoiding certain hayfever drugs, especially antihistamine's like Terfenadine, i.e. Triludan and also Astemizole, i.e. Hismanal in patients who may have heart or liver disease; and so on and so forth.

2. Is prescribing of a drug necessary?

The prescriber should always remember Hippocrate's edict "First, do no harm". A risk–benefit analysis should be done before a drug is prescribed. Examination of a patient should not necessarily be followed by writing of a prescription – explanation of the symptom to the patients *or* even education is all that may be necessary. In particular, antibiotics should not be prescribed unnecessarily, especially for viral infections. Indiscriminate use of antibiotics clearly increases the risk of bacterial resistance (please see chapter 8 on Infection in the Elderly).

3. Correct prescription-writing

Legible handwriting (e.g. writing in capital letters), correct amount of drugs prescribed, avoidance of abbreviations, correct instruction to take medicine (avoiding the instruction to 'take as directed') are some examples of good prescription writing. Pa-

tient's choice and convenience should not be forgotten – patients should be able to open the drug containers, child-proof containers should not be granny-proof.

4. Counselling about drugs

Clear cut instructions should be given to patients concerning;

a. How (say, by mouth,) how often (e.g. three times a day), roughly how long to take (e.g. 2 weeks, or 6 weeks etc.)

b. Any important side effect of the drug and what action to take if it happens.

c. Written instruction supplied if there is a complex drug regime (a copy of which should be sent to the patient's General Practitioner)

d. Extra care should be taken re: patients in nursing homes as several doctors visit these places. It is prudent to liaise with a lead person over there.

e. How to get drugs if the currect stock finishes. This is especially true for drugs like steroids, pain-killers, inhaler devices, drugs for treating diabetes, hypertension and heart failure (e.g. water tablets, digoxin). Help from neighbours, friends and relatives, homehelps and chemists is very welcome.

5. Compliance

Non-compliance (ability to comply with the instruction given by the prescriber of drugs) is a big problem, especially in up to one quarter of elderly patients. The reasons are multiple. The common causes being poor eyesight, forgetfulness, taking too many drugs already, poor physical health and fear of having drug side effects (the last may be due to poor explanation given to patients on necessity or the frequency of taking drugs). There are several ways to improve compliance.

a. Supervision by District Nurses or Seamless Pharmacist and help from friends and relatives in taking drugs.

b. Simplifying the drug regime, i.e.

i. taking a drug once daily, (if possible) instead of twice or three times a day,

ii. inhaler devices, insulin injections (say by PEN), *or* rapidly dissolving pain-killer tablets and putting in eye drops, can all be simplified appropriately.

c. Weekly drug container packs may also be used to improve compliance.

d. As mentioned above, patients must be given clear cut instructions concerning their drugs.

e. Drug monitoring (verbal checking; or even blood monitoring may be necessary in many cases e.g. lithium, drugs used in epilepsy, Digoxin etc.)

f. The policy of 'start low and go slow' should be adopted (drug doses should be built up slowly) in elderly patients.

g. Polypharmacy should be avoided, if at all possible (use dietary measures before starting cholesterol-lowering drugs). Elderly patients find it difficult to take more than three drugs a day.

h. Information leaflets should be supplied to patients.

i. Periodic review of drugs is necessary and repeat prescriptions should be scrutinised regarding drug-doses and indeed their continued uses.

6. Cost effectiveness of the drug

a. Resources should not be diverted to treatments whose clinical benefits and cost-effectiveness have not yet been proven. Even if a drug is effective, one should ask if it is clinically indicated in a patient – take for example, Viagra, now available on NHS prescription, though only in certain specified conditions.

b. It is cheaper to prescribe drugs by their generic names. Some drugs bought over the counter (O.T.C.) may be cheaper.

c. Specific examples of cost-effective prescribing include Warfarin for secondary prevention of strokes and heart attacks and combinations of calcium and vitamin D to prevent osteoporosis in patients in residential homes. In fact, as presribers,

doctors should have a rough idea about the price of a drug.

7. Medico-legal implications

a. Patients should be told about possible important side effects of the drug prescribed.

b. To consider use of another drug if side effects from a drug are expected after its protracted use in higher doses. It is well known that a daily dose of prednisolone for conditions like rheumatoid arthritis, asthma, temporal arteritis for more than 6 months, will increase loss in bone density with likelihood of fracture of the bones. However, this need not be so as the use of bi-phosphonates (say Didronel PMO) in steroid-induced osteoprosis reduces bone density loss (please also refer to management of steroid-induced osteoporosis in chapter 13 on Osteoporosis).

c. If there is doubt about the correctness of a prescription the prescriber should be and is contacted by the Pharmacist.

8. Prescribing in special patient groups

Elderly patients
Elderly patients are likely to have several medical problems and hence are on multiple drugs. Indeed, 45 per cent of all prescriptions are now for people aged 65 and above. For several reasons, drug handling in the elderly is different compared to in younger patients. This is particularly in respect of psychotropic drugs (i.e. sedatives, tranquillisers and anti-psychotic drugs).

Prescribing in pregnancy/women of child-bearing age
Although out of context here, it is worth mentioning that utmost care should be taken whilst prescribing drugs during pregnancy, more so during the first 3 months of pregnancy. The horrors of the drug Thalidomide (used in pregnancy as a safe sedative for morning sickness) are well known. (In 1961, it was found to cause severe malformation in

the foetus; it is now being used in leprosy (for leprous skin lesions after it was approved by Food and Drug Administration, in USA).

9. Precautions while prescribing new drugs including clinical audit (i.e. sharing and assessing medical information by a group of professionals)

Strict protocol should be followed for use of new drugs (as outlined in the British National Formulary which is revised twice a year). If necessary, further information about the drugs should be requested from manufacturer's product literature/ drug information units.

Clinical audit is now part and parcel of good medical practice as this focuses on maintenance of standard. No doubt audit on drugs (old and new), is already practised, it is the change in clinical behaviour which is needed after such audits.

10. Reporting of side effects

It is vital that doctors and hospital pharmacists report the side effects of drugs taken – both old and new drugs – to Medicines Control Agency CSM, Freepost, London, SW8 5BR. Clearly this measure will be of immense benefit to future patients. It is worth remembering that some drugs may take a long time to show their side effects. Practolol was withdrawn after several years of being prescribed.

11. Continuing medical education – The Eleventh Commandment

Attendance at medical meetings, discussions with colleagues, and keeping in touch with publications about disease management in journals and books, go a long way to keep us up to date with all aspects of medical care including drugs and their prescribing. Evidence-based medicine is becoming the order of the day, but this has to be practised with due consideration for individual patient's needs.

Final message

1. It is the scientifically proven view of a good clinician which is at the heart of a rational prescribing.

2. Once a decision to prescribe a drug has been taken, the prescriber has to take into account its efficiency, side effects (see no 3 below), cost, and last but not least, patient's convenience and choice.

3. A careful watch for possible side effects must be kept on all prescribed drugs, both old and new, but especially newly marketed drugs. Reducing drug side effects is not only the business of prescribing doctors but also drug regulatory authorities (by tighter control on licencing and drug-marketing), pharmaceutical industries (by marketing of safe, and cost-effective drugs) and pharmacists (by complementing doctors' advice to patients, scrutinising prescriptions and other measures such as checking, while dispensing systemic steroids, if the patient has a steroid-treatment-card, if not, to issue one, if appropriate, and inform the prescribing doctor about it).

Useful address

Royal Pharmaceutical Society of Great Britain
1 Lambeth High Street,
London SE1 7JN
Tel No: 0171 735 9141

References/Further reading list

1. *Pharmaceutical Medicine* (Eds. Burley, Clarke and Lasagna), 2nd edition (1993). Edward Arnold.

2. *Journal of the Royal College of Physicians of London*. Vol 31, May/June 1997.

3. *British National Formulary* No. 36 (September 1998), A joint publication of British Medical Association and The Royal Pharmaceutical Society of Great Britain.

4. *Caring for Older People* - edited by Eileen Burns, Neil Penn and Graham Mulley. (Series of 14 articles, published in *British Medical Journal*, between July 1996 and October 1996).

Medicine in the New Millennium

How to reduce side effects due to drugs ? The answer may lie in genetics. With the news that the human genome can be roughly sequenced within 3 years, individual patients will be able to have tailor-made medicine. Thus, the era of mass medicine (i.e. prescribing the same drug to everyone who suffers from the same disease) may be substituted by gene-specific therapy (i.e. patients will be prescribed drugs and lifestyles, such as diet, which will be in keeping with their gene types), so the 21st Century Medicine will not assume everyone to be the same.

[Source: *The Daily Telegraph* Sept 23, 1998]

Community Care – a Wider Picture

CHAPTER 20

Abbreviations used:

N.H.S. = National Health Service, D.O.H. = Department of Health, P.C.G. = Primary Care Groups, C.A.B. = Citizens Advice Bureau, G.Ps. = General Practioners, B.G.S. = British Geriatric Society, C.P.N. = Community Psychiatric Nurse, D.S.S. = Department of Social Security

The idea of Community Care is not new. This was thought of several decades ago. However, over the recent past there has been a significant change in the way elderly people are cared for in community and hospital settings. The emphasis has moved from hospital-based treatment and care to a more community-orientated service. In the past, a network of home support was provided for elderly people by members of their family who lived in the same locality. Changes in society have meant that in more recent times the close-knit communities have, in many instances, disappeared, and therefore, there has been a greater need for services to elderly people to be provided by the statutory and voluntary services.

The hospital-based 'long-stay' beds were supplemented by contracted beds in privately run institutions but these elements of care, which in many instances could be regarded as custodial, are now declining and emphasis is placed on people being allowed to choose the environment which best meets their own requirements and allows them to function to an optimum level of independence.

So, many 'long-stay' wards have been mostly removed from hospital and inpatient care is concentrated on acute and rehabilitation provision. Elderly people are cared for and maintained within the community in a variety of settings. These comprise of their own homes, relatives' accommodation, residential and nursing home placements and 'Retirement Homes'.

Emphasis should now be on maintaining elderly people in their own homes in the community and they should only be admitted to hospital when, like other people, they require hospital-based acute and rehabilitation care. Elderly people, however, in most instances present with multiple pathology and, therefore, have different demands on services compared to younger people. Thus they require a greater range of service. Every effort should be made to facilitate early discharge to an appropriate setting within the community. This should follow a well-structured plan which has had multi-disciplinary involvement from patients, relatives, NHS, Local Authority and appropriate voluntary services.

To understand the complex issue of Care in the Community it is important that at this stage we examine in detail the objectives, principle and various acts concerning community care: it is estimated that out of an elderly population of over nearly 9 million, one million of these people need assistance from others to help them to look after themselves. The vast majority of them rely on family members for that support but there are many who have no families able or available, to assist them or who have such complex needs that families cannot provide the necessary care. The State, throughout the centuries, has, through various Acts of Parliament, intervened in such instances. The NHS and Community Care Act 1990 extended and clarified those interventions and was intended to provide a framework for the assessment and support of people with disabilities and chronic illnesses and to shape the development of the community care services provided by both the NHS and Local Authorities.

The guidance paper, "N.H.S. Responsibilities for Meeting Continuing Health Care Needs" was subsequently issued in 1995 to help re-define the boundaries between continuing social care needs that required Local Authority intervention and continuing health care needs that remained the responsibility of the NHS. The Carers (Recognition and Services) Act of 1995 was also implemented to ensure that the needs of non-paid carers, if appropriate, would be addressed.

So what is community care?

According to the opening statement of the British Government's 1989 White Paper, 'Caring for people', 'Community Care' means providing the services and support which people who are affected by problems of ageing or mental illness, mental handicap, or physical or sensory disability need to be able to live as independently as possible in their own homes or in homely settings in the community'.

Community care principles

Having incorporated the above objectives, the NHS and Community Care Act 1990 established the right for people with significant disabilities and chronic illnesses: to have an assessment which identified their needs; to be allowed to make decisions for themselves based on comprehensive and accurate information; to be given appropriate choices across the statutory and voluntary and independent sectors; to have individual care plans produced, detailing services tailored to meet their personal requirements and to remain living in their own homes with all the attendant risks – (unless they fulfilled the criteria for admission to hospital under Sections 2, 3, or 4 of the Mental Health Act 1983 or Admission to Residential Care under Section 7 of the Mental Health Act 1983 or Section 47 of the National Assistance Act 1948).

Multidisciplinary/agency co-operation and assessment was considered to be the cornerstone of the Community Care process, with the added aim of achieving better integration of services within and between all agencies. Care plans were to be effective within available resources, efficient (encouraging continuity and with no duplication of services) and economic.

It was suggested that people who provide or supervise a hands-on service, may colour their assessments by their knowledge of staff/service availability (service-led). As assessments had to be objective and not led by resource implications, it was felt that people who purchased the service would be able to undertake such needs-led assessments more effectively. It was also suggested that budgets should be held as near to the client as possible to make the purchase of services less bureaucratic. Subsequent legislation gave Local Authorities the discretionary power to allow disabled people under the age of 65 years to be given the opportunity to arrange and purchase their own care services.

Local Authorities' assessments criteria

All Authorities have set criteria to dermine who is eligible for an assessment of need. Some people have a right to an assessment and these include:

- people who are blind or partially sighted, are deaf or hard of hearing, or people who have no speech;
- people who are substantially and permanently disabled by illness, injury, or a congenital condition;
- people who have a mental health problem or a learning disability;
- anyone who cares for a person with a disability or who is providing a substantial amount of care for a person needing community care services.

Other criteria are likely to include:

- people who are in danger of physical or emotional harm or abuse;
- people who are at risk of losing their independence;
- people who are unable to maintain a reasonable quality of life, with an acceptable level of risk;
- people who request residential or nursing home care;

Areas of need

Local Authorities were made responsible for assessing the following areas of need:

- personal/social care (Daily Living Activities);
- health care (physical, mental, emotional and medication);
- accommodation;
- finance;
- education/employment/leisure;
- transport/access;
- special needs, e.g. religious, cultural;
- carers' needs.

Assessments should be multi-disciplinary, if appropriate, and must be done in partnership with users and with carers (with the user's permission).

Health Authority assessments criteria

The Health Authorities were made responsible for the multi-disciplinary assessment, provision and funding of services for patients with any of the following continuing health requirements:

- continuing in-patient care under specialist supervision in Hospital or in a Nursing Home;
- a specialist medical or specialist nursing assessment;
- rehabilitation and recovery;
- palliative health care;
- respite health care;
- community health support services to people at homes, or in residential care homes;
- specialist health care and specialist support to people living at home, in residential and nursing care homes;
- specialist transport services.

Care planning and negotiation process

As assessment should have established the abilities of the user and identified the areas where the user required some assistance to achieve his/her optimum level of functioning. Needs should be met within available resources. Relatives, friends and neighbours are likely to be asked if they would be assisting to meet any of the users' identified needs.

Wherever possible the user should then be given information on all the existing, appropriate options available to meet any outstanding needs. These may include services provided by both statutory, voluntary and independent agencies. The care package should then be negotiated with the provider services and finalised. Users have the right to refuse services and to live at risk.

Various needs and who provides them?

The range of assistance is enormous and differs between Local Authorities. Informal carers, such as relatives, friends and neighbours, provide important services, from undertaking practical tasks to giving emotional and social support. Domiciliary care workers and Homemakers undertake both household and personal-care tasks; volunteers may undertake gardening and handyman chores, provide practical items or advocacy services;Luncheon Clubs and church groups provide social support and a listening ear; the University of the Third Age and other educational classes provide stimulation and leisure time activity; Housing Agencies, Associations and the Housing Department provide Wardens for reassurance or specially adapted housing or shelter for homeless people; Day Centres usually provide care and assistance often for those with fewer abilities; respite care offers relief for carers and residential and nursing home care offers full support for those unable to be cared for in their own homes. (It is worth pointing out that in general, there is a lack of regular social and recreational activities in nursing and rest homes. A lot could be done in this direction, without spending too much money, by some innovative ideas and also by involving many enthusiastic friends and relatives).

Social Workers/Care Managers assess, monitor, support and counsel users and carers, providing a pivotal role in negotiating, arranging and purchasing necessary services and also offer some protection from abuse. GPs, District Nurses, Community Psychiatric Nurses, Community Mental Health Nurses, Macmillan and Marie Curie Nurses provide direct health care, treatment, advice and support. Occupational Therapists assess for adaptations and together with Physiotherapists offer ongoing rehabilitiation for a variety of conditions and provide necessary aids.

Welfare Rights Agencies and CAB provide financial and legal advice whilst DSS and charities provide financial assistance.

Some concerns

The NHS and Community Care Act 1990 is generally considered to be a very good piece of legislation which should ensure that people in need receive a thorough and effective assessment of their needs and the risks to their health and well-being. However, it has been less than effective in some areas of the country due to lack of funding; increased expectations of users and carers; a huge increase in demand and inequality in provision.

Other causes for concern have arisen from the blurring of the boundaries between Health Authorities and Social Services Departments' responsibilities; changing policies, continued duplication of some service provisions; lack of joint planning and narrow, blinkered, – rather than holistic- approaches to developments.

The failure of some agencies' personnel to embrace the concept of Community Care, out of jealousy, resentment, loss of power, or lack of vision has led to conflict and sabotage by default.

Recent developments

The White Paper "The New NHS Modern, Dependable", Dec 1997 (See Appendix I) confirmed this Goverment's determination to reduce some of these causes for concern, by insisting on joint working and planning between the Local Authorities and Health Authorities. This can only be of benefit to Users and Carers, who ultimately do not mind who gives, organises, or manages the support services, so long as they receive what they need with the minimum of fuss and bureaucracy and preferably without having to go to too many places or speak to too many people.

Primary Care Groups

Needless to say 'Primary Care Groups' (PCGs) responsible for commissioning health services for the local population, are the foundation stones of the new NHS. As mentioned above, General Practitioners, Community Nurses, Social Services Staff and others will need to work together to provide services. To start with, a lot of flexibility will be needed in the size of PCGs. There will also be the need to find ways of securing effective participation by Social Services, Nurses and local people. Besides, to avoid mistakes, 'road testing' of the core components of the reform will be needed to achieve the best care in coming years.

Care of carers

The management of services for elderly people needs to pay greater attention to the role played by informal carers who provide a large element of support for elderly people in the Community. If they are to continue in this role then the statutory services need to ensure that immediate access to the appropriate level of respite care is available, now mostly in the community, i.e. in residential/nursing home. Where necessary this should be done on a regular basis.

The recent Government initiative, Caring for Carers, is a step in the right direction and should be welcomed – carers of patients (of all age-groups) are to be given £140 million spread over 3 years in England. This would enable the carers to take short breaks from their duties.

Royal Commission on Long-term Care

This long-talked about report is just out (March 1999). The Commission had made several useful recommendations (please see Appendix 2).

Ethical/management dilemmas

Mention should be made of the management/ethical dilemmas

1. Although it may seem to be basic advice, one thing is quite clear and that is whether the elderly patients are being treated in the hospital, the nursing home, or indeed in their own homes, it is the treating doctor's personal responsibility for advice regarding treatment – both regarding day-to-day management for common conditions, but more so regarding at the end of life situations, when living wills are brought into play. Doctors should not simply abdicate their responsibility and hide behind 'patients or relatives wishes'. It is, of course, entirely a different matter if patients choose to reject or refuse treatment to be given.

2. We have to learn from other professions as to how to strike a balance between cost and quality.

3. Priorities of the patients should be identified - we must learn how to assess the needs of our patients.

Care of elderly people from ethnic minorities (especially those with origins from Indian subcontinent and those who are Caribbean)

Elderly people from these ethnic minority groups, although they have a well-defined cultural background, they are not a homogenous group. As their number is going to increase in coming decades, it is essential that both hospital doctors and General Practitioners have some basic know-how of cultural background of these minority groups. Whether it is for acute medical treatment or screening of their various medical conditions (especially hypertension, diabetes, ischaemic heart disease, osteoporosis, dementia and depression), the doctor should in the first instance, be able to communi-

cate with them, either directly or through interpreters. These patients also need information leaflets in their own language. In some situations, especially while screening for dementia and depression, culture-specific tests should be used. Happily a good start has already been made in these
areas. This needs to be strengthened and continued.

Role of other bodies/organisations
Mention should also be made here of bodies like
the British Geriatric Society (it has suggested crea-
tion of a single purchasing authority responsible
for all aspects of elderly care), British Medical Association, Royal College of Nursing, Age Concern
and Help the Aged and other organisations. These
organisations/bodies either singly or in collabora-
tion with each other have been directly or indirectly responsible for improving the qualities of
life of millions of elderly people in the community. They deserve and need all the possible help
from the Government on one hand and the general public on the other.

Is 'Care in the Community' working?
It has to be accepted that problems in the care of
the elderly people – both medical and social – are
not straightforward in view of complex interplays
of factors, as mentioned above. It is, therefore, not
surprising to read the recent report on clinical
standards in the Advisory Group's Report that care
in the community for elderly people is not working well. There are two main reasons:
1. Community health and social services are described as fragmented, rather confused and un-
der-funded.
2. Some organisations are working differently, e.g.
Age Concern is working in different ways to improve access to and co-ordination of services.

All in all, good will and co-operation of all
concered is needed to improve the uniformity of
care provided to the patients in the community.

One hopes the latest extra NHS modernisation
fund to refurbish and re-equip the NHS during its
50th Anniversary Year (i.e. 1998) will go a long way
to improve these difficulties. But then "we never
shall have all we need" observed Aneurin Bevan
the founder of the NHS.

Summary

1. Need for integrated Service
We must aim for an integrated service-provision,
encompassing both primary (community) and secondary (hospital-based) care. Besides, there should
be more liaison between health and social services.
Ideally there needs to be an integration of these
two services.

2. Care should be comprehensive
Patients need both 'Therapeutic' and 'Prosthetic'
approaches to their care. The latter needs multi-
disciplinary involvement (e.g. meals, home care,
telephones, alarms, house adaptation, respite care
etc.) There should be close liaison between
various agencies providing care so that care could
be targeted to those who need it and that there is
no unnecessary duplication of services.

3. Long-term care
a. Patients needing long-term care should be medically assessed in case they have some treatable/
medical condition.
b. Local Authorities should provide adequate
financial information to those needing long-term
care.

4. In an effort to give 'incentive' to more and more
elderly people to stay in their own homes, Community Services should be strengthened. Indeed,
there is a need for a comprehensive National Housing Policy including innovative housing schemes
like Retirement Homes.

CARE OF THE ELDERLY

5. *Duties of Local Authorities*

Local Authorities legally need to carry out assessment of need and depending on this, decide the nature of care people need.

6. Physicians, especially specialists in the Care of the Elderly, should make themselves available for visiting elderly people in the Community – especially in Nursing Homes – as part of their contractual obligation (which may need negotiating) especially in the light of the sea-change currently taking place in the working of NHS.

7. *Support to carers*

Practical support to carers should be given priority. This is already being looked into.

8. As a long-term measure (e.g. to enjoy retirement years) it is prudent for every working man and woman to have adequate additional Pension provision from the beginning of starting their jobs.

Appendix I
White Paper December 1997
= The New NHS

Six principles are spelled out in the White Paper

1. Renewing the NHS as a 'genuinely national' service;

2. Making treatment delivery a local responsibility, with GPs and Nurses in the 'driving seat'.

3. Breaking down barriers in Health Authority Organisation;

4. Boosting efficiency through performance checks and cutting bureaucracy;

5. Guaranteeing excellence, with quality the 'driving force' for decision-making.

6. Rebuilding confidence in the NHS as an of accountable service.

Appendix 2
Royal Commission's Proposals on Long-term Care (March 1999)

1. All nursing and personal care to be free to all those who are assessed as needing it.

2. Saving level to be raised from £16,000 to £60,000 (including value of a home) before a person has to start paying for their own care.

3. Normal living and housing costs would remain the responsibility of care-home residents.

4. For up to three months after admission to care in a home, the value of a person's home should be disregarded to ensure that people are able to return to their own home if needed.

5. Opportunity for rehabilitation as part of care-assessment.

6. Integration of budgets shared between Health, Social Services and statutory bodies.

7. Local Authorites allowed to make loan to individuals needing aids and housing adaptations

8. Introduction of National Carer Support project to help carers.

9. Delaying illness and dependency on long-term care by preventive medicine and health education.

All in all, the elderly may not have to sell-up to afford care.

[Source: *The Times*, March 2, 1999]

Useful addresses

1. **Research Institute for Care of the Elderly**,
   St. Martin's Hospital,
   Coombe, Bath, Devon BA2 5RP
   Tel 01225 835866

2. **Disabled Living Foundation**,
   380–384 Harrow Road,
   London W9 2HU
   Tel: 0171 289 6111

3. **General Medical Services Committee**,
   British Medical Association,
   London WC1H 9JR

(This committee represents all National Health Services General Practitioners)

References/Further reading list

1. *Lecture notes on Geriatrics* (Ed. Nicholas Coni and Stephen Webster Blackwell Science Fifth Edition, 1998.

2. Primary Care and the NHS White Papers Editorial, *British Medical Journal*, June 6, 1998

3. *British Medical Journal*, 11th July 1998 issue.

4. *British Medical Journal* 24th January 1998 issue.

5. Making Primary Care Group Work - Editorial, *UPDATE for General Practitioners* 8th April 1998 issue.

6. Book Reviews - *British Medical Journal* 11th April 1998.

7. *The Sunday Telegraph* May 31, 1998.

8. *Potential for Health* by Dr Kenneth Calman. Oxford University Press (June 1998).

9. *Health Care* for *Older People* (by Steven Iliffe, Linda Patterson, Mairi Gould. BMJ Publishing House, ISBM 07279 11929.

11. *The Coming of Age – Improving Care Services for Older People*. Audit Commission Report, (Published October 1998.)

10. *Assessing Health Needs of People from Minority Ethnic Groups* (Ed. Salam Wafaf and Veena Bahl) ISBN 1 86 016 0581 Softer cover 1386 Pages.

12. *From Cradle to Grave (Fifty Years of the NHS)* by Geoggrey Rivett, Kings Fund, January 1998.

13. Community Care for the Elderly People. Editorial, *British Medical Journal*, 19 August 1998 552–553

Acknowledgement

I am very grateful to Mrs Dorothy Phillips of the Social Services Department at The Royal Oldham Hospital for her considerable contribution in the preparation of this chapter.

Picking Care Homes
for the Elderly

Facts and figures

1. Average cost £352 a week for a nursing home and £252 a week for a residential home.

2. Under the present system, people who move into a residential or nursing home pay all costs if they have savings (including the value of their home, if living alone) of £16,000 or above. If their savings drop below £10,000 the state pays the whole bill.

3. While nursing home placement takes place through health authorities, residential home residents can choose between homes in their area and these are regulated by local authorities. There is thus a possibility of couples splitting if one needs residential care and the other nursing home care.

4. There is no proper well regulated official advice and support to relatives concerning choice of accommodation for their patients.

5. It is important that apart from looking for clean accommodation, relatives must ask specific questions from staff and also see if other residents are happy, the place is easily accessible, staff are cheerful and above all, the place is welcoming. A useful book which answers all these questions is *Home from Home*, available from King's Fund Bookshop and costs £5.95. Tel: 0171 307 2591.

6. Some 40,000 people a year have to sell their homes to pay for long-term care. Many consider this an injustice that they should have to use their savings, having been prudent all their lives compared to those who pay nothing and have not bothered to save.

[Source: *The Times*, October 8, 1998 and February 27, 1999]

Final Reading List

(especially for Doctors and Senior Nurses)

1. *A Guide to Care of the Elderly* (Eds. R.B. Shukla and D. Brooks) HMSO Books, 1996.

2. *Principals and Practice of Geriatric Medicine* (Ed. M.S.J. Pathy) 2 Volumes 0471 963 488, John Wiley and Sons, May 1998.

3. *Brocklehurst's Textbook of Geriatrics and Gerontology* (Eds, R.C. Tallis, J.C. Brocklehurst and H. M. Fillit) 5th Edition, Churchill Livingstone. January 1998, 0433 053707.

4. *Medicine in Old Age* (Ed. Stephen C. Allen) Churchill Livingstone, 4th Edition, Feb. 1998.

5. *Older People, Nursing and Mental Health* by several authors. Butterworth Heinemann, August 1998.

6. *Cancer – Principals and Practice of Oncology.* (Eds. Vincent T Devita, Jr. Samuel Hellman and Steven A. Rosenberg) 5th edition 1997, Lippincott Raven.

7. *Horizons in Medicine* No. 8 (Ed. Michael J. G. Farthing), Royal College of Physicians of London. (arises from R.C.P.'S 1996 Advanced Medicine Conference - Published Sept. 1997). I.S.B.N. 186 016 0689.

8. *Oxford Textbook of Palliative Medicine*. Eds. D. Doyle, G.W.C. Hanks and N. MacDonald, October 1997. 0-19-262- 566-7

Some Useful Publications by Age Concern

(Information and specialist advice for the over 50s and those working with them. Address: Age Concern England, Astral House, 1268 London Road, London SW16 4ER. Tel: 0181 679 8000 Fax: 0181 679 6059)

1. Passport 50 Plus – a Practical Guide to the Law in England and Wales. Citizenship Foundation, June 1998, 160 pages, 034 071 1884. Price £3.99

2. Elder Abuse – Critical Issues in Policy and Practice (Eds. Phil Slater and Mervyn Eastman) January 1999, 160 pages, 086 242 2485, Price £14.99

3. Nutrition of Older Adults (Dr. Geoffrey Webb and June Copeman) 176 Pages, 03 40601566, 1996 (Price £13.99)

4. Business Skills for Care-Management – a Guide to Costing, Contracting and Negotiating (Penny Mares). 144 Pages, 086 2421918, 1996 (Price £11.99)

5. Promoting Mobility for People with Dementia – a problem solving approach (Rosemary Oddy). 144 Pages, 086 2422426, Sept. 1998, (Price £14.99)

6. The Retirement Handbook (Caroline Hartnell). 208 pages 086 242 237 x Oct. 1997 (Price £7.99)

7. Caring for Ethnic Minority Elders – A Guide for Care Workers (Yasmin Alibhai-Brown). 144 Pages, 086 242 1888 May 1998, (Price 14.99)
00325848

Index

Printed in the United Kingdom for The Stationery Office Limited
J71840 C8 4/99 9385 9814